The Diversity Agenda:
Lessons and Guidance from the Legal Profession

EDITED BY FRANCESCA RAMADAN

Head of events and books
Leah Darbyshire

Commissioning editor
Alex Davies

Editorial assistant
Francesca Ramadan

Published by
Globe Law and Business Ltd
3 Mylor Close
Horsell
Woking
Surrey GU21 4DD
United Kingdom
Tel: +44 20 3745 4770
www.globelawandbusiness.com

ISBN: 978-1-78358-326-3
A catalogue record for this book is available from the British Library

Contents

Executive summary

In 1913, in a case that became infamous, a judge at the British Court of Appeal ruled that women were not considered "persons" and were therefore not entitled to become practicing lawyers. Times have certainly changed since then, and progress is being made in terms of the inclusion of women and other minorities. However, it is still very much the case that lack of diversity – whether that is in terms of age, faith, social mobility, gender, disabilities, sexual orientation, and ethnicity – remains a problem in the legal profession. Indeed, a worrying trend identified in recent years has seen percentages of minorities entering and progressing within the profession either stagnating, decreasing, or showing no significant improvement. In the latest bulletin released by the National Association for Law Placement in February 2018 on women and minorities at law firms, statistics show that the percentage of female associates in 2017 sits below its 2009 level and that growth in the share of African-Americans among associates has been virtually non-existent, peaking in 2008 and followed by a seven-year decline.[1]

Considering the current sociopolitical climate, these figures may come as a surprise. Indeed, in both law firms and other businesses, the conversation around organizational diversity is in many ways more fervent, active, and engaged than ever before. Prominent figures in the profession make bold declarations about their belief in the positive contribution increased diversity brings, and firm websites are not considered complete without a visible commitment to improve their inclusivity. It would seem that everyone is aware of the problem, and is vociferous about their attempts to tackle it. However, the numbers show that the needle is barely moving. The legal profession appears to be stuck at the point of discussion, and the measures that have thus far been implemented – which typically include token changes in company policy and written charters and agreements – can more resemble posturing than steps to achieve real change. The challenge, then, for any law firm which recognizes that diversity is a force for innovation and seeks to genuinely make a change, is finding those actions that do make an obvious and measurable difference. What can be done, and where does one find the practical advice needed to instigate the change?

Packed with constructive guidance and compelling insight from industry experts and thought leaders, *The Diversity Agenda: Lessons and Guidance from the Legal Profession* seeks to provide the answer to these questions. Moving past the identification of an obvious problem, this book will instead offer effective solutions to those endeavoring to maximize their firm's potential through the benefits diversification can bring. *The Diversity Agenda: Lessons and Guidance from the Legal Profession* aims to supply a unique perspective from authors who have experienced institutional challenges and obstacles, providing proactive steps to take in order to negotiate them. Expert advice is also supplemented by real-world examples of pragmatic, effective, and award-winning diversity initiatives that are being pioneered by both international and regional law firms.

In chapter 1, Rosalie Chamberlain – principal of Rosalie Chamberlain Consulting & Coaching, a consultant, leadership coach, and speaker, and former diversity and inclusion Manager of an AmLaw 100 firm – looks at how bias drives negative reaction to the issue of resistance to diversity. She explains the importance of connecting diversity to organizational needs, and that while diversity is a stated focus for the legal industry, inclusion is where the rubber meets the road. She explores the role of inclusive leadership and how understanding privilege can be a catalyst to positively impact organizational inclusiveness.

It is easy to identify a lack of diversity in a firm; the difficulty emerges when trying to establish what the next steps are and what exactly a more inclusive workplace might look like in terms of what it offers to its employees. Chapter 2 sees Sharon E. Jones – an internationally recognized expert and consultant on diversity and inclusion and the legal profession – lay out the key components of a successful inclusion strategy, beginning with the means with which one can measure organizational diversity and moving onto policies and programs that can be implemented to foster and embrace diverse talent.

The team at Hogan Lovells believe that people are at their best when they can be themselves – working together and delivering for their clients. In line with this commitment, the firm has launched a unique trans inclusion initiative, ensuring its trans and transitioning people and the teams they work in are given adequate guidance and support in the workplace. In chapter 3, Ruth Grant – award-winning litigation partner at Hogan Lovells International LLP and a member of the Hogan Lovells board – outlines the background and context of the award-winning initiative, its coverage and impact, and what happens next.

Both psychological and physical ability are often behind the curve when organizational diversity initiatives are discussed. In chapter 4, Yasmin Sheikh – founder of Diverse Matters, a consultancy specializing in disability issues, and former lawyer of 12 years – explores the reasons behind this before proceeding to utilize both her professional expertise and her personal insight as a wheelchair user to offer techniques that bring disability firmly back onto the diversity agenda.

What motivates people to be their best selves when it comes to their work is different for each individual, and in chapter 5, Karen G. Johnson-McKewan – partner at Orrick, Herrington & Sutcliffe, named one of the 100 "Most Influential Women in Bay Area Business" by the *SF Business Times*, and a top female litigator by the *Daily Journal* – argues that the legal profession is missing what drives women to be successful, which accounts for their absence in the higher echelons of firm leadership. Fusing personal insight and quantitative data, Karen maintains that it is passion that firms must aim to inspire in their female lawyers in order to ensure greater rates of engagement and retention.

In chapter 6, Wesley D. Bizzell – senior assistant general counsel for Altria Client Services and president-elect of the National LGBT Bar Association – tackles the issue of being LGBTQ in the legal profession and presents ways in which firms can build opportunities and create pipelines for their staff of differing sexual orientations. Drawing from both his professional expertise and his personal experience, Wesley outlines methods for implementing cultural change and asserts that establishing an open and welcoming working environment is the first proactive step a firm can take. Pragmatic guidance is offered by Wesley with regard to creating conditions in which both employee and wider organizational authenticity is key.

The evidence has repeatedly shown that "diversity 101" – those initial, tentative measures taken by firms thus far to improve their inclusivity – isn't working. In chapter 7, Reed Smith partner Daniel Winterfeldt delves into the origin and mechanics of the Apollo Project, a global cross-sector initiative for organizations which provides the practical tools needed to better embed more inclusive workplace practices and cultures to promote meritocracy. The Apollo Project – which is an offshoot of the Interlaw Diversity Forum, of which Daniel is founder and chair – seeks out ground-breaking examples of best practice which are backed up by evidence, and then offers these as an "open-source" resource. Some past winners will be highlighted as inspiration for best practice in cultural change, providing a template that can be adapted for different organizations.

Many firms will state their commitment to greater inclusivity and accessibility, but few will actually put in place schemes that command significant resources and input in order to guarantee it. Garden Court Chambers, a leading UK firm based in central London, is the exception. Its pioneering program "Access to the Bar for all" – which won Diversity Initiative of the Year at the 2017 UK Diversity Legal Awards – moves past the traditional one-week shadowing scheme format and aims to tackle the issues faced by young people from underprivileged backgrounds by providing long-term guidance and support in the form of extensive mentoring and funding. In chapter 8, Charlotte Ogilvie, marketing and communications executive, delves into the mechanics, context, and impact of the scheme, providing an inspiring and compelling example for others to follow.

Discerning consumers and top talent increasingly wish to see their values, including support for LGBT+ inclusion, expressed by companies. CEO activism and backlash against the LGBT+ community are both on the rise. As opportunities for businesses to engage on public policy in support of LGBT+ equality multiply, and as corporate leaders face internal and external pressures to act, how can they most effectively decide when and how to proceed? In chapter 9, Todd Sears – founder and principal of Out Leadership, the global LGBT+ business network CEOs trust – discusses how his firm engaged a working group of business leaders from across a spectrum of industries to understand how leading companies evaluate these choices and make decisions, in order to formalize a set of guidelines intended to help businesses of all kinds engage productively and beneficially on LGBT+ equality.

Reference

1. "Women and Minorities at Law Firms – What Has Changed and What Has Not in the Past 25 Years", *NALP Bulletin*, February 2018. Found at https://www.nalp.org/0218research [accessed 16 March 2018].

About the authors

Wesley D. Bizzell serves as assistant general counsel, external affairs and director of political law and ethics programs for Altria Client Services LLC. Overseeing a comprehensive compliance system covering the regulation of government affairs, Wesley provides advice and guidance on political law compliance for more than 75 jurisdictions. Wesley is extremely active in promoting diversity and inclusion within the legal and corporate communities, and is an active member of several of his organization's equality groups and the chair of its Culture, Inclusion and Connection Committee. In 2017, he was named by the *Financial Times* as one of the 100 OUTstanding Leading LGBT+ Corporate Executives, and is a board member for the National LGBT Bar Association, having also recently served as its president-elect.

Rosalie Chamberlain is the director of Rosalie Chamberlain Consulting and Coaching. She is a skilled leadership and executive coach and consultant, having worked extensively with clients in the legal industry, as well as a broad range of corporate, government, and private industries. She served as the diversity and inclusion manager for a national AmLaw 100 firm prior to starting her own consulting and coaching business. Rosalie has more than 18 years of experience working with individuals and groups on leadership development and talent management. She is a member of the Committee for Diversity and Inclusion of the National Association of Legal Administrators (ALA), and is featured as one of several selected Top Lawyer Coaches, powered by Diversity Lab. She is also the author of *Conscious Leadership in the Workplace: A Guidebook to Making a Difference One Person at a Time*, which addresses authentic leadership, with a strong focus on the impact of biases.

Matt Fouracre is the manager of client relations and public policy at Out Leadership, where he oversees client relationships with Out Leadership's member companies around the world and leads public policy efforts. Prior to joining Out Leadership, Matt worked as a congressional staff assistant and constituent service advocate for former US Senator Mark Udall. Matt received an MA in International Relations from the University of Chicago, with a research focus on international political economy. He earned a BA in International Studies from the University of Denver, and spent a year in the War Studies Department at King's College London."

Ruth Grant is a litigation partner at Hogan Lovells International LLP and a member of the Hogan Lovells board. Former London managing partner and firm people development partner, she chairs Hogan Lovells' Global Diversity and Inclusion Committee. She is a member of the SRA Equality, Diversity and Inclusion Committee, the WILEF Global Advisory Board and the City of London Law Society Training Committee. She has a particular focus on recruitment of BME and socially disadvantaged graduates and the progression of women and LGBT lawyers in the profession. Ruth received the 2012 Association of Women Solicitors Award for Best Woman Solicitor Retaining and Developing Legal Talent and won "Woman Lawyer of the Year" at The Law Society Excellence Awards 2016. In 2016 she also won the Black Solicitors Network's Diversity Champion Award.

Karen Johnson-McKewan, a partner at Orrick, Herrington & Sutcliffe in San Francisco, specializes in litigation that crosses the boundaries between traditional legal practices. For more than 30 years, she has first-chaired state and federal trials, and arbitrated more than a dozen disputes. She manages intellectual property and commercial matters for companies such as Oracle, NVIDIA, Netflix, VMWare, and Levi Strauss & Co. She has been named one of the 100 "Most Influential Women in Bay Area Business" by the *SF Business Times*, one of the "Top Women Litigators" by the *Daily Journal*, and won the National Association of Women Judges' Florence K. Murray Award for leadership. Most recently, Karen has been named to *The Hollywood Reporter's* 2018 Power Lawyers list for her work on behalf of Netflix.

Sharon E. Jones is an internationally recognized expert, consultant, author, and speaker on diversity and inclusion, unconscious bias, and the legal profession. She is the author of *Mastering the Game: Career Strategies for Success* (2018), designed to explain the unwritten rules for successfully navigating large corporate workplaces for women, minorities, and other diverse individuals. Sharon is also the president of Jones Diversity, Inc., a diversity and inclusion consulting firm which works to create an inclusive workplace culture. Sharon has practiced law and been a community leader for over 25 years, including positions as a federal prosecutor, with major law firms and with Fortune 500 Corporations. Sharon is a past president of the Black Women Lawyers Association of Chicago and is a graduate of Harvard Law School and Harvard College with a degree in Economics.

Charlotte Ogilvie is the marketing and communications executive at Garden Court Chambers a high-ranking UK barristers' chambers based in central London that is committed to human rights, social justice, and equality. She is a first-class History graduate from the School of Oriental and African Studies, University of London, and has worked across a variety of communications and editorial roles internationally from Bangkok to Amman.

Todd Sears is the founder and principal of Out Leadership, a global business advisory that connects leaders across the world's most influential industries to create business opportunities, cultivate talent, and drive LGBT+ equality forward. Todd began his career as an investment banker before moving to Merrill Lynch to become a financial advisor, where he created the first team of financial advisors on Wall Street to focus on the LGBT community. He then moved into diversity leadership, pioneering equality initiatives first at Merrill Lynch and then at Credit Suisse. Sears serves on the non-profit boards of the Williams Institute of UCLA, The Palette Fund, the Global Equality Fund of the United States Department of State and Lambda Legal, and is a graduate of Duke University.

Yasmin Sheikh is the founder of Diverse Matters, a consultancy specializing in disability issues (both visible and non-visible disabilities) in the workplace. She is also the vice-chair of Lawyers with Disabilities Division (LDD) at the Law Society and also Council member representing LDD. Yasmin helps organizations empower their workforce to be disability confident through her consultancy services, workshops, coaching, and disability-focused events. She is a multi-award-winning speaker at the Professional Speakers' Academy and speaks regularly about diversity with a particular focus on disability at many large organizations. She is a former lawyer of 12 years; having acquired her injury in 2008, she is now a wheelchair user. Yasmin packages her experience, expertise, and knowledge to deliver informative and transformative workshops and events to both employees and employers to become more confident when it comes to diversity and disability.

Daniel K. Winterfeldt is a partner at Reed Smith and a US securities lawyer with over 18 years of experience, with his practice focusing on representing investment banks and corporate issuers in a wide range of securities transactions. Daniel is also the founder and chair of the InterLaw Diversity Forum, through which he has spearheaded the ground-breaking *Career Progression Report in the Legal Sector*, the Apollo Project to promote business cultural change, and the Purple Reign initiative, which highlights LGBT and straight ally role models and multiple identities. He was named the "Legal Innovator of the Year" at the *Financial Times*' Innovative Lawyers Awards in 2012 for his work in capital markets and diversity and inclusion.

Chapter 1:

Where the rubber meets the road – tackling resistance to diversity

By Rosalie Chamberlain, consultant, leadership coach and speaker, and former diversity and inclusion manager of an AmLaw 100 firm

The likelihood that individuals in firms and legal departments wake up in the morning thinking, "Who can I marginalize or discriminate against today?" is extremely unlikely. However, while many of these organizations state that diversity is a core value, they have not yet achieved the level of diversity that reflects a significant change in the demographics of the workforce and especially the make-up of the leadership. On top of the ongoing challenge to create more equitable organizations, there is continued "resistance" to focusing on diversity in the legal profession.

Resistance

To examine the matter of this resistance, let's look at the definition. According to the *New Oxford American Dictionary* and the *English Oxford Dictionaries*, resistance is: (1) "the refusal to accept or comply with something; the attempt to prevent something by action or argument" and (2) "the ability not to be affected by something, especially adversely". What does resistance to change efforts mean with this definition in mind?

Resistance as a refusal to accept something is a result of basing one's thoughts on opinions rather than facts. The National Association for Law Placement's recent analysis indicates that "although women and minorities continue to make small gains in their representation among law firm partners in 2017, the overall percentage of women associates has decreased as often as not since 2009, and the percentage of Black/African-American associates has declined most years since 2009, with small increases only in 2016 and 2017."[1] We can't change what we don't see, and refusing to see the facts highlighted in numerous studies is an opinion that does not help in creating change.

Resistance shows up in many aspects of life – specifically, regarding changing habits and preferred ways of doing things. Resistance is often based on bias, which is defined as "a cause to feel or show inclination or prejudice for or against someone or something". As we know, we all have biases; whether they are explicit or implicit, they drive our decisions, behaviors and choices on a daily basis. If we reflect on the definitions of resistance and bias as behaviors that keep the diversity and inclusion needle from moving, a deeper dive is needed into understanding the "why" there is a struggle for increasing diversity in organizations.

Diversity and organizational goals

Much has been written about the business case for supporting diversity and inclusion initiatives. The client demand is not a secret. The fact is that we live in a global marketplace. Yet, staying with the status quo (a bias that drives many leaders and organizations) is detrimental to increasing diversity. The marketplace is not standing still. The search for talent and the need to recognize, maximize, retain and advance talent is always moving and very competitive. Ultimately, the economics are affected when a firm has high attrition and the advancement of under-represented lawyers is low. When lawyers who want to advance believe they do not have a path to contribute, perform meaningful work, and excel because the opportunities do not exist, they leave. There is a cost to the firm in the immediate sense, and there is a cost to the future attraction of talented lawyers because the "word on the street" reflects a lack of diversity and inclusion.

Once someone is at the firm, there needs to be more focus on development and advancement. If the focus is strongly on retention through development and advancement, attracting and recruiting can then produce long-lasting results. Firms and organizations often get it backwards. They hire top talent and then – because of multiple cultural factors including bias and outdated policies, procedures, and attitudes – some of that talent falls through the cracks.

Some of the usual excuses made for a lack of inclusion are the issues of lack of time in a high-stakes environment, which translates into sticking with the same choices for staffing matters; a client's request for specific individuals; uncertainty; discomfort; and again, staying with the status quo. It may be easier and more efficient, but it is not doing much to move the needle for diversity.

The basic need is for inclusion, which is where the rubber meets the road if an organization wants to attract, develop, retain, and advance the best of the best. Even among the firms and legal departments where diversity is a stated core value, equitable inclusion is not an automatic practice. Imagine the image of a tire on the road. Next, look at a tire with snow chains that provide safety and protection but do not allow all of the rubber on the tire to meet the road. This analogy fits many organizations that value diversity yet are not fully there. What if we remove the chains of resistance? To do that, we must commit to recognizing biases and their impact. This applies to all individuals within the organization.

What's fear got to do with it?

Why is inclusion so challenging? An important factor influencing the advancement of women lawyers, lawyers of color, LGBT lawyers, and lawyers with disabilities is fear. I am not talking about real life-or-death fear, but fear of not meeting the clients' needs, of competition, of not reaching their own path to success, the general high risk of stepping out of what is tried and true, and fear of not knowing what to do. All of these factors mean that it can indeed feel like life or death to the individual in some cases.

There is often great resistance towards examining biases, both because there is fear of looking or feeling badly about oneself and fear of change. For example, if I risk putting "you" on the team and you do not perform as I want you to, it then reflects on me – what will happen to my hours, compensation, etc., if I advocate and include you? These types of thought patterns are based on biases that often go unchallenged. In the immediate moment, excuses are made to stay with what is familiar, with what is the most convenient or efficient way of doing things. There is an underlying and often unconscious belief that it is safer to stay with the usual procedures.

Research in neuroscience addresses the brain's automatic associations. "The amygdala is the emotional center of the brain that reacts to fear and threat and other senses… The amygdala isn't the only part of the brain involved in unconscious bias. The frontal cortex is also identified as important in forming impressions of others… Memories such as dates and fact, also subconsciously steer people toward choosing one option over another."[2] These internal unconscious biases influence every decision we make. Moreover, if a memory includes a negative teaching or interaction, the tendency is to rely on that memory to inform our current situation about what might be true. However, the fact is that it might not be true.

Exploring these habitual beliefs requires a thought-provoking challenge to break them down for understanding. I address using the acronym of F.E.A.R.© in a recent TEDx Talk and in my book *Conscious Leadership in the Workplace: A Guidebook to Making a Difference One Person at a Time*. I pose five questions that anyone can use to examine a bias (belief):

1. What is the specific belief?
2. Where did I learn it?
3. Is it true (specifically, do I *know* it to be true in this situation)?
4. What do I *choose* to believe?
5. What action(s) can I take?

To further examine fear and break it down to discover what might lie behind it, the following framework can be utilized to help someone recognize and understand and hopefully move past their fear. We must start within to understand our own journey and be willing to experience discomfort.

- F – We experience a sense of **fight or flight** and feel a strong need to defend – position, status, self-esteem, or whatever we are afraid of losing or confronting – or withdraw from the situation or person entirely. There is need to pause, observe our thoughts and the potential impact;
- E – We **exclude.** We exclude others and separate because of experience, or what we have been told or taught;
- A – We **avoid**. We avoid possibilities, opportunities, building relationships, ways to collaborate, and learning something new. We try to avoid tension, discomfort, or uncertainty; and
- R – We **react** instead of effectively responding. Split-second, habitual reactions are a result of our brain's unconscious mental shortcuts to make some sense of our world.

The commitment to recognize, identify, and examine one's beliefs by pausing with conscious awareness is a game changer. One may still make the same choice in the end, depending on the situation, but does so with conscious awareness and understanding. This approach does not take away someone's "power" to choose, put someone on a team, promote them to a position, etc.

Backlash and resistance motivated by fear is evident when someone does not know what to do or how to do it, and wants to stay in their comfort zone. Unless a person thrives on creating change and challenging the status quo, it is not necessarily going to be comfortable. Studies reflecting that diverse teams outperform homogeneous teams have existed for a while, and yet still there is some resistance to these facts.[3] An underlying reason for resistance may be that, when working within diverse teams, there is often a natural discomfort with dealing with varying perspectives, and the ability to resort to "group think" does not make the process as comfortable. Thus, getting out of the comfort zone and deciding to be open to diverse perspectives will help achieve the best outcome. Understanding these thought processes can help normalize fears. Most people do not like to admit fear, but when thoughts and feelings are normalized, it helps.

Too few leading the way

Another resistance-creating behavior in many firms and organizations is that the diversity and inclusion efforts are left to a "few" (diversity committees/councils, HR, champions), which can be overwhelming. How can a partner or senior associate meet the demands of the high stakes, fast-paced work environment and still be responsible for inclusion efforts? Where is the time, ability or bandwidth when it is only on a few? The inclusion efforts need to be woven into the fabric of the entire organization. Business development, professional development, marketing, finance – all departments of the organization need to have a diversity and inclusion lens. Implementing a strategy to have someone from each of the administrative departments and management committees as a representative on the diversity committee/council can ensure the firm or organization is not making decisions that are more exclusive than inclusive.

As an example, recent ads have been challenged because of stereotypes which are often offensive. I recently read a piece highlighting a new *Star Wars* Monopoly game that – despite the fact that the last installments of the *Star Wars* movies have had female heroes as main characters – had not one single female character represented in the initial game. Really? Who was at the table for that decision? The bottom line is that the decisions and the processes put in place in firms and organizations must have a diverse perspective of voices at the table. If this is not happening, mistakes happen, and this too is costly. The "siloed-nature" of many diversity and inclusion efforts makes it more complicated. Expanding and building a culture of inclusion throughout the organization will make it less so. It takes work and time.

Inclusive leadership, bias, and individual responsibility

Inclusive leadership is critical to setting the tone for organizations and firms. Inclusive strategies need to be a part of organizational goals. Leaders need to clearly articulate desired outcomes, as well as identify the current state of the organization. Understanding the current state of demographics and inclusiveness is the first step in the process to measure progress as policies and procedures are put in place. Progress is not going to be made as a theory in a few minds, but rather by way of concrete plans and actions. While inclusion must come from the top, it must also come from the bottom up and across the entire organization. How everyone interacts and makes decisions about inclusion and exclusion has an impact. However, while intent may stem from a positive mindset, the actual impact may not equal the positive intent.

With respect to individual responsibility for inclusion, there is often too much focus on "them" doing something different. Could it be that there is only a cursory acceptance or understanding of the impact of bias (conscious and unconscious)? Could more personal commitment and willingness to be part of the solution make a difference, instead of inaction and possibly remaining part of the problem? To create change in the level of inclusiveness of the organization, it is crucial for individuals to take personal responsibility. Albert Einstein once said, "Insanity: doing the same thing over and over again and expecting different results". Another apropos quote attributed to Einstein is, "The measure of intelligence is the ability to change". Which approach do you prefer?

Effective and sustainable change for creating an inclusive environment requires action and movement. The status quo will not get you where you need to be. So, let's examine some myths (traditional stories) that either stop or slow progress in advancing diversity and inclusion, and actions to take to be a part of the solution.

Myth #1: this is our model – the way we have always done things – and we are successful.

This translates into we either don't know how to or don't want to change. My question is: how is that working? It may work in some ways, but a closer look at the ability to attract, develop, retain, and advance top talent in your industry is impacted. Competition is strong and being an employer of choice is largely related to having a culture of inclusivity and equitable opportunity. Consider exploring "risk versus consequence factors" to determine what is best for your organization. Even if you are risk averse, what are the consequences of remaining with the status quo, and what are the consequences of working toward more inclusivity?

Myth #2: unconscious bias "training" does not work.

As we know, everybody has biases which have an impact on decisions that directly advance or stagnate progress in creating positive change.

Many people acknowledge that they have unconscious and conscious bias. However, many more choose not to look deeper at their own biases and how they impact everything, including the organization and their own careers. Another reality check is that unconscious bias training does nothing *if* only done as a "check the box" endeavor and there is no individual, personal responsibility to take the information and become aware of personal biases and their impact on others and oneself. Offering unconscious bias classes is a waste of time if all you do is say, "I've had that class" and walk away and do nothing. The quality of the class is extremely important, and the true onus lies with the individual in achieving understanding of what their biases are and how they influence beliefs, decisions, and actions. Without that, people do not create equitable systems, and once again one is stuck with the status quo. I understand people don't automatically change just because they become aware of a bias if they don't want to change a belief and behavior. However, if within the organization the expectation is to support teamwork, collegiality, and organizational goals and objectives that provide a more equitable and inclusive environment, it may require "parking" a belief to contribute to an environment where everyone will have the opportunity to succeed.

An effective workshop on bias is one where participants explore something that has been "scary" to look at and come away feeling curious and eager to examine further; where they have revelatory experiences, yet do not walk out feeling badly about themselves. I have witnessed both responses: "check the box" and taking personal responsibility and accountability. Individuals in the organizations that are committed to inclusivity take on the latter.

Myth #3: leadership development and effectiveness is for top leaders – it is their responsibility.

Leadership effectiveness is a two-way street. As stated by Rosamund and Benjamin Zander in their bestselling book, *The Art of Possibility*, you can "lead from any chair". True success requires individuals taking charge of their careers and being full contributors. The organization needs to be aware and examine policies, procedures, practices and systems and the inclusiveness of its culture, but individuals make up the culture and directly affect inclusion and performance. The organization benefits in countless ways when those in leadership positions work on how they show up every day. Engagement, motivation, and innovation are direct byproducts of effective leadership that contribute to performance excellence. However, don't think for a minute that it is only up to a few in the designated positions to make the difference. Everyone needs to step up and see how they are contributing and effectively leading their own career.

The partnership between an organization and the individuals within it is critical for success. All too often, one decides in advance how someone will respond or interact in a situation, which closes off potential. How can one really see someone if one has already decided how they will be? I have seen many coaching clients on the edge of missing opportunities because of blame and judgment of self and others. Blame has no place in leadership. A good rule of thumb is to challenge yourself when you hear yourself think or say: "if only they; if only it; if only I; if only he; if only she, etc". By doing so, we maintain the opportunity to effect change, growth, and more productive outcomes.

For years, in workshops and in relationships with clients, we have addressed individual responsibility for biased habits and behaviors that negatively and positively impact some and not others. Whether one falls on the side of denying that biases exist and have impact, or on the side that is committed to finding ways to mitigate biases, "bias is woven through culture like a silver cord woven through cloth. In some lights, it's brightly visible. In others, it's hard to distinguish. And your position relative to that glinting thread determines whether you see it at all."[4] A look at the habitual beliefs that drive everyday behaviors must take place if there is any intention to address the lack of inclusion in the legal profession.

Privilege as a catalyst for inclusion

We would be remiss to look at resistance to diversity, inclusion, and examining bias and not address the topic of privilege. Discussion of rank and privilege is not yet an everyday topic. In fact, it is often avoided as it can stir up a multitude of feelings and emotions. It does, however, need to be discussed. Prior to one of my speaking engagements on understanding rank and privilege, I overheard someone say they were not going to participate because it would be too heated. It does not have to be heated and contentious, and it was anything but; participants left the program with a deeper awareness and understanding of themselves and others.

There needs to be a willingness to explore what rank and privilege mean to each of us. There is a tangible impact even when the discussion is avoided, because denial of its existence creates barriers that separate and perpetuate systems which exclude. At the very least, the ability to positively impact inclusion is severely hampered. The *intent* to support equal opportunity for everyone is not enough, because there is a huge difference in equal opportunity and true equity.

> *"Equity and equality are two strategies we can use in an effort to produce fairness. Equity is giving everyone what they need to be successful. Equality is treating everyone the same. Equality aims to promote fairness, but it can only work if everyone starts from the same place and needs the same help."*
>
> (Amy Sun, 2014).

Herein lies the problem. Not everyone has equal access to what is needed for a fair opportunity. Realizing this difference and exploring where it takes place is an important step in creating change. Understanding the problem is not enough; taking action is required. Here are three things to keep in mind in exploring privilege:

1. **Examining privilege should not and does not need to make us feel guilty or ashamed.** Guilt and shame can be paralyzing and halt progress. Looking deeper can fuel our inner desire to be change agents and helpful, by understanding how our advantages can contribute to changing rules, procedures, practices, and laws that are potentially inequitable. An explorative mindset, without defensiveness, is an entryway into transforming exclusivity into inclusivity. We get out of the silos privilege has created and build community and purpose;
2. **Exploring our privilege does not mean we did not work hard or earn a certain position in life, career, and community**. Privilege allows for some to have advantages that others do not have access to just because of possessing "Major Identity Markers" (MIMs), which is what is often visible when we walk in the door. MIMs include race, ethnicity, gender, class, physical and mental ability, sexual orientation, religion, etc. The thought of making changes to remove access barriers often feels threatening because of a belief that *we* will lose something. This is a very dualistic view of the world or situation; it is an "either/or" attitude. Changing this to a "both/and" approach will promote collaboration to come up with ways to create equity; and
3. **Our willingness to show up, open and ready to have dialogue (not debate)** about this issue is a message we send whether we know it or not. A conversational dialogue may not be perfect, but that is not the point. A colleague and friend shared with me a

> quote that is very powerful: "You are not responsible for your first thought; but you are responsible for your second thought. Which choice will you make?". Understanding that our unconscious biases and beliefs drive our thoughts and behaviors helps give us space to pause, providing a little slack on the first thought, and allowing us to challenge the source and the truth of the automatic response.

One of the best ways privilege can be used to advance diversity and inclusion is when the influence we have can be utilized as a sponsor or advocate for others. It is necessary to include the input of all who are impacted in the discussion and efforts to promote inclusion. White males often have the most influential position in firms and legal departments, and their ability to create change and promote inclusion is dependent on their being included in the conversation. When the power that comes with privilege is used to support equity, the systems, policies, procedures, and behaviors in the firm or legal department can become more equitable.

Conclusion

Inclusion requires having continual awareness to create a powerful, engaging environment, and realizing that growth – both for the individual and the organization – is a natural part of that dynamic. An inclusive leader understands that people are the organization's assets, and it takes commitment to focusing on inclusion and addressing resistance to create a partnership that results in cultures of excellence. Inclusion promotes engagement, which inspires motivation and innovation. It is not a one-person show. It takes individual, as well as corporate, responsibility to make a difference. It takes letting go of resistance.

References

1. *2017 NALP Report on Diversity in US Law Firms*. National Association for Law Placement 2017.
2. Luskin, Bernard J., Ed.D., LMFT, 'MRIs Reveal Unconscious Bias in the Brain', *Psychology Today*, 2016.
3. Hunt, Vivian, Layton, Dennis, and Prince, Sara, *Why Diversity Matters*. McKinsey & Company, 2015.
4. Nordell, Jessica, 'Is This How Discrimination Ends?', *The Atlantic*, 2017.

Chapter 2:
Structural equity – key strategies for a successful inclusion initiative

By Sharon E. Jones, internationally recognized expert on diversity and inclusion and the legal profession

It is commonly recognized that a diverse and inclusive organization is important to successfully compete in the global marketplace in which we all work – whether we are competing for top talent, clients, the best product innovations or the best ideas and work product. Although much progress has been achieved, we still have miles to go before we can say we have created truly diverse and inclusive organizations. What is often missing is a focus on structural change. Organizations don't become diverse and inclusive without *attention* to structural changes within the organization and the *intention* to make structural changes sustainable in the long term. Structural equity is a focus on leveling the playing field for diverse individuals. This focus is on intentionally providing equitable opportunities for all. It helps to make the workplace culture more structurally inclusive and to keep employees engaged and productive.

This chapter addresses six structural change strategies which will create a platform for a successful diversity and inclusion initiative. These are:

1. An inclusion scorecard;
2. A program of unconscious bias education/training;
3. Formal mentoring programs;
4. Formal sponsorship programs;
5. Parental leave policies; and
6. On-ramping and off-ramping policies for people transitioning from parental or other planned leaves.

Implementing all six of these strategies will create a long term sustainable platform for your diversity and inclusion initiative. It will also help address common challenges with retention and advancement which are the most difficult challenges to overcome.

Inclusion scorecard

In our consulting work, we like to start with an inclusion scorecard. It creates an agreed upon way to measure where your organization is with respect to representational diversity and what your goals/benchmarks are. It can also directly impact hiring and advancement by bringing attention to these metrics. The legal profession is filled with people who are competitive and who want to achieve agreed upon organizational objectives. Therefore, the inclusion scorecard can be effective in motivating the organization to focus on key metrics. Tying compensation to the achievement of your inclusion scorecard goals is a way to turbo-charge the inclusion initiative.

Creating an inclusion scorecard that measures several subjective (non-diversity related) but important organizational goals is a great way to implement the measurement of diversity metrics which may be new to your organization. For example, in a law firm, you may want to measure the hours spent on pro bono projects/matters or the time spent on firm committees and other non-client, but important work. The inclusion scorecard can be used to include these important metrics as well as diversity and inclusion-related objectives. Measuring this type of non-client work is essential for the advancement of women and minorities. According to a recent research study, women and minorities routinely are asked or obligated to work on matters (such as recruiting, diversity, and other administrative tasks, etc.) for which no billable hour's credit is given (and no compensation is given), yet the work is needed by the firm.[1] Doing this work without credit or compensation does not lead to their professional success or retention.

So, what should your organization measure from an inclusion standpoint? First, it is important to examine hiring at every level. What percentage of your organization is represented by lawyers of color? What percentage is represented by women? LGBTQ lawyers? Lawyers with disabilities? At a minimum, the scorecard should help you track what is going on. What is the trend line? Are the numbers going up or down from year to year? To take your inclusion scorecard to the next level, you can track how the organization is performing against benchmarks or goals you have set. For example, the percentage of women or racial and ethnic minorities who graduate from law school is published yearly. In the US, information on women law school graduates is available from the National Association for Law Placement (NALP) and information on racial and ethnic minority graduates is available from the American Bar Association.[2] These are important benchmarks to have in your scorecard.

Your hiring numbers for new law school graduates ought to mirror the graduation rate or be very close to those numbers. This doesn't require your firm to change your hiring criteria. However, it may require your recruiting department to be more targeted in its outreach or to consider applicants from different law schools or to be more aggressive in your recruiting at the usual schools targeted. It often requires a realistic analysis of the schools at which your organization routinely recruits. What percentage of the graduating class is racially/ethnically diverse? Often, firms will realize that the schools at which they recruit aren't the best places to meet diverse candidates. The scorecard and analysis of the benchmarks in the scorecard assist you in reaching these important realizations.

Later, when you are ready to deal with another layer of the hiring data, you can analyze the recruiting process to see what the applicant pool is like when initial screening is conducted and what it is like at each level of the process. All things being equal, we expect to see the same percentage of women and minority candidates at each level of the hiring process – from screening interview to final offer. If you are losing candidates disproportionately along the way, it is important to identify the phase in the process where the loss occurs and to address it. Often unconscious bias/implicit bias is the cause of lost applicant candidates.

Regarding advancement, it is important to have metrics which demonstrate the number of underrepresented people in the group up for partner or other promotion. Intentionality regarding the consideration of diverse candidates is particularly important at this stage. The success of the "Rooney Rule" in the National Football League in the US has demonstrated the importance of diverse slates when decisions are made for important promotions/hiring. The Rooney Rule (named after the owner of the Pittsburgh Steelers) required each team to agree to interview at least one diverse candidate whenever they were going to promote/hire a coach or assistant coach. Over the years, this practice dramatically increased the diversity of the coaching leadership in US football teams. The Rooney Rule is now being applied in corporations and law firms to women and racial/ethnic minorities – both groups who are underrepresented in the legal profession.

There are any number of important metrics you can track to measure progress regarding diversity and inclusion and to provide an early warning system if the trend line becomes negative. The important thing is to begin and each year or two add additional metrics to the scorecard as the organization becomes comfortable with the concept. Focusing on these key metrics will keep your organization on course for a more diverse and inclusive culture.

Unconscious bias training

Unconscious bias, also known as implicit bias (used interchangeably herein), is a fundamental challenge facing most organizations. It is difficult to identify and to train people, but it must be addressed. Unconscious bias affects many aspects of an organization's operations and it must be disrupted on three levels: 1) individual; 2) team; and 3) organizational. Training can be effective to make people aware of unconscious bias and to provide some behaviors which create more inclusive diverse teams. However, it is also important to disrupt unconscious bias at the organizational level by creating structural changes. Formal mentoring programs and formal sponsorship programs, discussed below, are examples of structural changes designed to "level the playing field" and create a more equitable workplace culture.

For unconscious bias training to be most effective, it needs to be conducted in person in small groups where the participants have a chance to talk about issues and concerns as well as time to consider their own mental frameworks. Ninety-eight percent of our thoughts are automatic, so people need to intentionally take time to more carefully think about issues where they are aware unconscious bias is prevalent.[3] Awareness of the problem and interventions through structural change are essential in reducing the implicit bias that diverse individuals often encounter daily.

Formal mentoring programs

It is well established these days that mentors play important roles in the professional development of their mentees/proteges. Mentor relationships have historically developed organically – primarily though affinity bias. Affinity bias refers to the tendency of people to favor members of their own group. In organizations dominated by white males, it is often difficult for women or other diverse professionals to develop mentoring relationships because affinity bias is working against them. There aren't many people there who may naturally have affinity for these diverse professionals. Formal mentoring programs provide a way to ensure that at least every new employee has a chance to have a mentor to provide the unwritten rules to success at the organization as well as other key information.

These formal mentoring programs are even more important in the time of #MeToo, with concerns about sexual harassment and other inappropriate behavior between men and women. Formal mentoring programs provide a sanctioned reason for the relationship to develop and a structure for where, when, and how often meetings should occur. I have heard several men express unwillingness to organically develop mentoring relationships with women in the new #MeToo era, but a willingness to do so within the constructs of a formalized mentoring program.

Formal mentoring programs should match people across lines of difference. By so doing, the organization is creating opportunities to build multi-cultural competencies while providing important mentoring to diverse professionals. The training should provide ground rules for the frequency of meetings as well as share some topics for discussion. Participation should be monitored and surveyed on a real time basis so that relationships that are not working can be dissolved and new relationships created. Mentoring programs are important to the success of women and diverse professionals. In the busy world in which we work, these relationships won't develop without time and intention from your organization's leadership.

Formal sponsorship programs

Sponsors are essential to advancement in today's organizations. Sponsors differ from mentors significantly. Mentors do not have to be people of power or influence. On the other hand, a sponsor is a person of power and influence who is in the room when important decisions are made regarding promotion, advancement, or special opportunities and he or she advocates on behalf of his/her protégé. Without a sponsor, it is extremely difficult, if not impossible, to reach the highest leadership roles in most organizations, whether that is partner, managing director, vice-president or higher. Reliance on sponsorship relationships to develop organically has been unsuccessful for most diverse individuals. According to recent research, men are 46 percent more likely than women to have a sponsor advocating for their success.[4] White professionals are 63 percent more likely to have a sponsor than professionals of color.[5]

Formal sponsorship programs designed to match diverse individuals with powerful sponsors and to create opportunities for sponsorship relationships to thrive, over a specific period, have been successful in advancing women and racial/ethnic minorities. Usually, sponsorship program opportunities are offered to people after they have worked at the firm for several years. This type of program supports structural equity and can assist in improving retention and advancement for women and other diverse professionals.

Parental leave policies

Providing flexibility to employees to care for their families is a major retention-focused strategy regardless of gender. Maternity leave policies which historically focused only on the birth mother have evolved in the most progressive and inclusive companies to parental leave or family leave policies. These policies treat leave for child care purposes equally for women and men. They also treat caregivers the same whether the employee is the primary or non-primary caregiver. These policies also are available regardless of how the child came to the family – through birth, adoption, surrogacy, or other family additions. Therefore, these parental leave policies cover both gay and straight parents and parents regardless of gender. Recent research shows that women progress better in workplaces where both women and men have access to and take parental leave as opposed to workplaces which fail to value men/fathers through leave policies.[6] Even more progressive are policies which include people who have elder care responsibilities as well. These policies recognize the aging population base and that employees often have elder care responsibilities in addition to parental responsibilities. Creating a family friendly environment that is gender neutral is a great strategy for increasing retention of high-potential employees. Both men and women value these policies and interpret the workplace culture based on the presence or absence of these family friendly policies.

On- and off-ramping

Another family friendly policy involves on-ramping and off-ramping – namely policies designed to smooth out the transition between leaving for a parental leave and returning after the leave. Usually, in a law firm, as a person approaches the parental leave date, they may find that they don't have any work to do long before they need to leave the firm. That can be demoralizing. When the person returns from leave, the options are usually no work for many months after the return or too much work when the person needs to ease back into work after a parental leave. Depending on the family situation and support at home, the employee may need to work part-time for a few weeks or months after returning. Policies which expressly allow for this type of flexibility are viewed as very family-friendly and promote long-term retention by working with the employee when he/she needs it most. In implementing this type of policy, a lot of work must be done with law firm partners and other leaders to teach them how to support the on-ramping/off-ramping policies as opposed to thwarting this new initiative.

An additional supportive option is to provide group or individual coaching assistance in work/life integration for employees returning to work after a leave as part of the on-ramping process. This can be very valuable in making the return a success. The loyalty that employees have after receiving this type of support from an employer is significant.

Conclusion

Each one of the strategies described above will improve your workplace culture. Successful implementation of all the structural equity strategies will significantly improve your culture and address the challenges of retention and advancement of diverse professionals. By being intentional about diversity and inclusion and giving it your attention, your organization can achieve a long-term sustainable inclusion initiative.

References

1. Joan C. Williams and Marina Multhaup, "For Women and Minorities to Get Ahead, Managers Must Assign Work Fairly," *Harvard Business Review*, 5 March 2018, accessed 6 April 2018, https://hbr.org/2018/03/for-women-and-minorities-to-get-ahead-managers-must-assign-work-fairly.
2. National Association for Law Placement: Recent Graduates (https://www.nalp.org/recentgraduates).
3. American Bar Association Statistics: JD Enrollment and Ethnicity (http://www.abarequireddisclosures.org/)
4. The Implicit Association test is a good way to test your own implicit bias. Go to www.implicit.harvard.edu.
5. Sylvia Ann Hewlett, *Forget a Mentor, Find a Sponsor: The New Way to Fast-Track Your Career* (Boston: Harvard Business Review Press, 2013), 24, 209-10.
6. *Ibid.*
7. Ellyn Shook and Julie Sweet, "When She Rises, We All Rise. Getting to Equal 2018: Creating a Culture Where Everyone Thrives," *Accenture*, accessed 6 April 2018, https://www.accenture.com/t20180307T184141Z__w__/us-en/_acnmedia/PDF-73/Accenture-When-She-Rises-We-All-Rise.pdf, p. 13.

Chapter 3:
Ahead of the curve – trans inclusion at Hogan Lovells

By Ruth Grant, partner and board member of Hogan Lovells and receiver of the 2016 "Woman Lawyer of the Year" and "Diversity Champion" awards

At Hogan Lovells, we believe we are at our best when we can be ourselves – working together and delivering for our clients. In line with this commitment, we launched a unique trans inclusion initiative ensuring our trans and transitioning people and the teams they work in are given adequate guidance and support in the workplace.

Diversity and inclusion are at the core of who we are and how we do business. We recognize our success as a global firm depends on our ability to attract and retain the brightest, and to foster a work environment where people of all backgrounds and experiences can reach their full potential. Our approach aims to ensure Hogan Lovells remains a diverse and inclusive place to work, free from workplace hostility and discrimination, and we are proud to be ahead of the curve for our comprehensive approach to trans inclusion.

Being trans inclusive is an essential element of how we interact with our clients, candidates, and people. We have long championed transgender rights in the workplace and have represented transgender rights clients on a pro bono basis on several occasions. In order to progress this agenda, we launched what we believe to be the UK legal sector's first Gender Transitioning in the Workplace Policy, which provides details of the support the firm offers to any of our people who wish to transition and to the teams with whom they work. To complement the policy, we also provided our people with trans inclusion training.

This initiative was partially driven by an incident which occurred during an event we hosted for an external LGBT+ organization. A member of our security team, which is provided by an external supplier, accidentally mis-gendered a trans guest at this event. This experience prompted us to ensure our client-facing teams are better equipped and supported to understand trans issues and interact with trans guests and colleagues.

Our additional motivations for launching the trans inclusion initiative included ensuring our employees are not confronted by workplace hostility, poor awareness, or lack of support. We wanted to ensure that Hogan Lovells remains a diverse and inclusive place to work and demonstrate to trans employees that they are an important part of the organization and that we offer guidance and a safe workplace for them should they wish to go through the gender transitioning process. Other objectives included supporting colleagues of trans employees, raising awareness of trans inclusion more broadly, and increasing confidence and understanding when interacting with trans people both inside and outside the workplace.

Background

At Hogan Lovells, we have a long history of championing LGBT+ inclusivity. Our UK Pride Network was launched in 2007 as the London LGBT Network and was re-branded and re-launched in 2012 as "Hogan Lovells Pride" to renew our focus on creating an LGBT+ friendly environment and demonstrating the contribution of LGBT+ professionals to legal and business services.

The mission of our Pride Network is to make a positive contribution to the lives of our members, Hogan Lovells generally, and wider society by ensuring Hogan Lovells is an environment that is LGBT+ friendly, not just LGBT+ tolerant. We achieve this by creating and maximizing business opportunities through LGBT+ connections; raising the profile of Hogan Lovells as an LGBT+ inclusive business; being a popular, active, supportive, and fun network for LGBT+ people and those interested in LGBT+ issues at Hogan Lovells; and providing support, information, and advice on LGBT+ issues for colleagues throughout the firm. Our Pride Network's Steering Committee is chaired by a partner and has members from across the firm, both LGBT+ employees and straight allies. The Steering Committee is responsible for driving the agenda and coordinating related internally and externally focused events and activities throughout the year to build the profile of the network and Hogan Lovells as a proud employer.

However, despite the network's active Steering Committee and full program of activity, we had a noticeable lack of focus on trans inclusion issues, so in 2015 we decided to address this head-on.

Getting started

In order to galvanize support, our Pride Network began by holding a lunchtime talk, open to everyone in the firm, as part of our "Different Perspectives" speaker series with Juno Roche, a leading trans rights campaigner.

Juno is a former primary school teacher who taught for eight years before she decided to transition. She has been featured in *The Independent*'s Rainbow List, which is an annual celebration of the lesbian, bisexual, gay, and transgender people who make a real difference in Britain, and she was a "Blair Peach Award" winner in 2015 for outstanding contribution to equalities.

During her talk, Juno shared her transitioning story to a packed room of employees from all levels and areas of the firm. She discussed the legal battle and other challenges she has faced as well as the issues she believes still need to be addressed within trans politics and legislation. The event encouraged our employees to openly discuss trans inclusion. It was very well-received, and feedback from the talk showed the appetite for more trans inclusion work:

> *"It was a privilege to hear Juno's story first hand. I learned a lot from her and from the questions asked. Along with her great courage and persistence in pursuing her personal journey, I was struck by her passion and commitment to her teaching career."*

> *"'Powerful and a tremendous insight into the issues."*

> *"Overall it was very informative. She said at the beginning she wanted us to see her as a human being first. And she succeeded. She's a brilliant woman and it was a very informative speech."*

Our Pride Network used the momentum from Juno's talk to develop a gender transitioning policy.

The policy

To begin work on the policy, we invited Juno back in to host a Q&A session with members of our HR team representing areas including advisory, operations, recruitment, and benefits. The HR team was prepped to ask any questions relevant to their areas in order to assist in drafting the policy and considering what other policies and processes would also need to be adapted. Following this session, an HR working group was formed to create our Gender Transitioning in the Workplace Policy.

The policy is designed to ensure appropriate support is provided for transitioning individuals and their colleagues, and it outlines guidelines for transitioning gender in the workplace, including information on what resources and guidance the firm can offer. It is important to recognize that these are only guidelines, as there is no single formula for managing transitions in the workplace and we recognize that every transition is different.

The policy begins with a statement on our commitment to trans inclusion.

Policy statement

> *"We are fully committed to supporting any of our people who wish to transition and recognize the qualities and strengths required throughout this process. The HR team and management will offer the appropriate support to ensure that the work and personal wellbeing of our people are maintained throughout the transition.*
>
> *Inclusion and wellbeing are at the core of who we are, and we respect our people who identify as trans. We recognise that our success as a global firm depends on our ability to attract and retain the brightest, and to foster a work environment where people of all backgrounds and experiences can reach their full potential. We will not tolerate discrimination or adverse treatment of any employee who identifies as trans or is intending to transition because of their trans status."*

Additional sections of the policy cover:

- Points of contact that can provide confidential support and answers to questions;
- Tips for the transitioning individual, their manager, team, and the firm's recruitment teams;
- Communicating the transition, including confidentiality and advice on communicating to colleagues and clients and other external contacts, both in terms of educating and employing appropriate language;
- Practical considerations including time off for medical appointments and changing room facilities;

- Updating records and systems including payroll, benefits, and pensions; and
- Recruitment of transitioning employees.

The policy also includes a gender identity glossary and a pronoun guide.

Through the policy we also encourage each individual who is transitioning to create a plan in consultation with their supervisor and/or HR representative which should be reviewed throughout and after the transition process. The plan is designed to assist in ensuring a smooth transition process, anticipate any potential problems, reduce uncertainty, and provide all people involved with a clear set of steps and timeframes to follow. As part of the policy, we provide an action plan template which includes a list of things to consider, and sections for recording timelines and key milestones, a stakeholder list, records and system updates, pronouns and name changes, and any necessary adjustments.

Once drafted, the policy was reviewed and approved by members of our Pride Network as well as our employment law team. We launched it internally in our weekly all-staff email as well as with an external press release.

Trans inclusion training

While drafting the policy, we worked with Rachel Reese of trans inclusion consultancy Global Butterflies and a trans representative on the Law Society's LGBT committee to develop and deliver bespoke trans inclusion training for our client-facing teams (including external suppliers such as security staff), HR, and our recruitment team.

The training covered gender identity and trans terminology, the gender transitioning process, practical considerations, advice on how to communicate with our people and clients using appropriate language, trans inclusion in recruitment and HR, and the trans inclusive workplace.

The training proved to be highly successful, with very strong and positive post-training feedback from attendees. Following this success and due to repeated requests, we added several additional training sessions which were opened up to everyone in the firm. These were also well-attended and received excellent feedback.

Our trans inclusion training reached over 100 people in total, with more than 90 percent of attendees rating the training as excellent or good. Attendees also commented on the changes they would make as a result of attending the training:

- "Review current practices with the mind to be more inclusive to the trans community";
- "Be more understanding"; and
- "More conscious of my language and have this more front of mind."

Additional employee feedback on the training included:

- "I think it's important that the session is delivered by someone who has been through this change as employees may never have met anyone who has transitioned before. Rachel is highly informative, inspiring and very entertaining, which put us all at ease and made the session enjoyable."
- "Putting training into real life context to help give an understanding what an individual has to go through was helpful."
- "I think this topic is important, and I'm glad that as a firm we take inclusion of all people so seriously."
- "As a result of meeting Rachel, I would actually feel more comfortable around trans people in the future knowing that they just want to be accepted and treated normally."
- "If it could be delivered more widely to increase awareness I think that would be a good thing."
- "This was an exceptional course. I hope that this will be offered more widely."
- "Just want to say again what an exceptional session this was. Everyone I've spoken to has said the same – thank you for running this."

Impact

With these initiatives in hand, we have received external recognition for our work, including coverage in *The Times*, *Legal Cheek*, and RollonFriday. Our approach to trans inclusion was also a key factor in us receiving our highest ever ranking of 17 in the Stonewall Workplace Equality Index in 2017, our first time in the top 20.

In addition, we have had a number of clients and other external organizations contact us asking us to present and share best practice on our work, allowing us to leverage and deepen client relationships through this initiative.

Internally, we have reaped a number of benefits including promoting a true culture of inclusion, through understanding, respect, and openness to current and prospective employees and empowering our people by giving them confidence in dealing with trans people, particularly for those in front of house roles.

The success of our trans inclusion initiative was highlighted in feedback from a transitioning employee:

> *"It was very reassuring for me to know that Hogan Lovells has a formal policy and network of support for transitioning. I decided to come out as transgender after a presentation on our diversity and inclusion. This is the first place I have worked that gave me the confidence I needed. Hogan Lovells has provided amazing support throughout my transition, for me and for my colleagues. In many ways, being surrounded by people that understand and support transitioning is as important as my own personal challenges. If my experience is any measure, the policy has been an outstanding success."*

Next steps

Building upon the success of the trans initiatives, in May 2017 we launched our global Pride+ Network, the firm's first global Pride & Allies Network across all of our more than 40 offices. The Network aims to demonstrate the firm's solidarity and ensure that within the confines of the communities in which we operate, our lesbian, gay, bisexual, and trans colleagues are respected, embraced and supported, wherever they are in the world. There has been great interest in joining the network and becoming an ally, and we have specifically sought trans allies for Pride+. In less than a year since launching, employee membership has reached over 1,300 members.

In addition, our UK Pride Network has continued to drive the trans inclusion agenda. We are in the process of reviewing and updating policies to ensure they are gender identity inclusive and have already made changes to our HR systems to ensure they offer an inclusive list of gender identity selections. In January 2018 we also hosted a Different Perspective talk by Jacqui Gavin, an award-winning trans role model and civil servant. Jacqui featured on the Pride Power List in 2016 and 2017 and has won awards such as "Highly Commended Diversity Champion – Public Sector" at the Excellence in Diversity Awards 2015 and "Diversity Champion" at the British LGBT Awards 2016. Jacqui shared her story along with tips on how to be a good ally, trans issues throughout her career and across different generations, and the importance of diverse strands working together.

We are tremendously proud of what we have achieved as one of the first in the market to bring the issue of trans inclusion into the mainstream.

Tips for the transitioning individual

- Inform key people in the firm who can assist you such as your supervisor and a member of your local HR team. Work with others to ensure they understand the process and your needs.
- Keep in mind that colleagues may not be educated about trans issues and therefore may not understand what your needs or concerns may be. The HR team can assist you in providing support and guidance and help you prepare for any discussions.
- Create a plan for your transition in conjunction with your supervisor and the HR team.
- Clearly state how you would like your transition to be communicated to colleagues and clients, including levels of confidentiality.
- Agree to schedule regular review meetings at key stages throughout the process.

Tips for supervisors, the HR team, the transitioning individual's team, and the recruitment team

- Listen and show support; seek advice and information from the HR team.
- Be open-minded and act sensitively when discussing the intentions, needs, and concerns of the transitioning individual. Remember that these can be very difficult conversations for a person to have with their supervisor.
- Agree on levels of confidentiality and ensure you maintain this confidentiality at all times.
- Allow the person to educate you on the transitioning process.
- Adopt an approach that meets the individual's needs and agree with them what steps need to be taken before, during, and after their transition.
- Create a plan in conjunction with the individual and other key people, for example members of the HR team.
- Agree to schedule regular review meetings at key stages throughout the process.

- In general, it is considered insensitive to continue to refer to someone by the wrong pronoun once you have established which pronoun(s) they prefer. Deliberate and/or persistent use of the wrong pronoun(s) can be considered discrimination or harassment under the Equality Act 2010.

Chapter 4: Disability, a desirable disadvantage

By Yasmin Sheikh, consultant and vice-chair of Lawyers with Disabilities Division (LDD) at the Law Society

When diversity and inclusion in the workplace is talked about, are people with disabilities thought of? I will be examining in this chapter why disability is often behind the curve and is overlooked when organizational diversity initiatives are discussed. I will also share my techniques/tips on bringing visibility to it and the reasons why disability should be firmly on the diversity agenda. The complexities of addressing disability will also be discussed – when you think about disabled people, is the association of simply sticks and wheelchairs? What about non-visible disabilities and long-term health conditions?

What is a disability?

A person is considered disabled under the UK Equality Act 2010 if they have a physical or mental impairment that has a "substantial" and "long-term" negative effect on their ability to perform normal daily activities.

This definition can include conditions such as cancer, dyslexia, and diabetes and is much wider than people think, as it includes both visible and non-visible disabilities/long-term health conditions.

Many people are probably unaware that they come under the umbrella of the legal definition of disability, which is one of the reasons for non-disclosure. Amongst those that are aware, their condition may be manageable and does not impact their work; there is therefore no reason to inform their employers.

My story

Most people, who do not have an experience of disability, and perhaps many employers also fall into this category, assume that someone with a disability comes with extra baggage, cost, awkwardness, and time. To put it simply, they are an inconvenience to the business.

The truth is that there is sometimes just a simple workplace adjustment which puts the disabled person on a level playing field and accepts that they may work in a different way.

Following a spinal stroke at 29, which meant I had to use a wheelchair to get around, I returned to work and had mixed experiences with people in the workplace.

One boss, who we called Clueless Keith, said to me: "The thing is, Yasmin, if I employed everyone with your disability, the business would collapse. In fact, I've got the same problem with part-time women workers. If I employed all of them, the business would collapse too." Keith didn't really grasp the concept of diversity – diversity of thought and the skills that different people can bring to the workforce.

The problem was that I believed him, as my confidence was low at that point after being off work for over a year. My belief was so strong that now as a chair user I was damaged goods, not able to contribute and participate fully in working life as I had done before – Clueless Keith just confirmed this. The funny thing was that as a lawyer I usually would require evidence to back up my beliefs. Despite the fact that I did not know anyone in a wheelchair, my belief was that my life would be limited, hopeless, and unfulfilling. In this, I was wrong.

What follows now are the things I wish I had said to Clueless Keith 10 years ago; however, at the time I did not realize my own strengths and had not encountered the many disabled people I have had the pleasure of meeting on this rollercoaster of a journey called life, including my husband who is also a wheelchair user.

There are many reasons for employing people with disabilities. Three main ones include:

1. Problem solving

In the early days after my injury, everyday tasks seemed difficult. How do I dress and wash myself? How do I get on a bed, or even carry a cup of tea? My legs stopped working and my head had to take over. Disabled people must always find a way to get around problems. There is a lesson that can be learnt here from the financial crisis and the groupthink that took place, with dire results. We need to attract different people with new solutions to problems.

Many people have never heard of the social and medical model of disability, and the differences between them. I hadn't either, but when I learnt about them it completely changed the way I looked at my disability.

The medical model begins with the premise that the disability is the problem. Disabled people need fixing; their bodies, senses, and minds are damaged somehow and impaired. As we manage our bodies in environments not built for them, the social barriers can sometimes be more awkward than the physical ones. Confused responses to racial or gender categories can provoke the question "What are you?", whereas interrogations regarding disability usually consist of "What's wrong with you?"

The social model completely turns that on its head. It says that what is disabling is not the disability itself but the attitudes, the infrastructure and environment that a person faces. If those barriers are removed, there is then no disability.

I say to clients I am coaching to think of their mind like Google. How can I do this, who do I know, what resources do I have and how can I get around that? People with disabilities are usually very resourceful, as we have to find effective and creative shortcuts that others haven't thought of.

2. Leadership skills

In a recent article in *Lawyer 2B* it stated that lawyers are less well-suited to leadership roles, which was measured by their ability to handle difficult situations and cope with uncertainty.

Disabled people deal with uncertainty all the time. Will a ramp turn up at the next station? Will this venue be accessible to me? How will this person react when I use the disabled toilet for my non-visible disability?

There is also a lot of discomfort around disability. Should I say something? Does she need a push? Is it rude if I say nothing? For this reason, people with disabilities need to take a lead to help others with this discomfort.

There are some that argue that events such as the Paralympics have demonstrated to the general public that disabled people can do amazing things. This is wrong. Research in the UK has shown that unconscious bias – prejudice towards a particular group of people – has increased towards disabled people since the London 2012 Paralympics. Disabled people tend to be polarized in the media, painted as either entirely reliant on welfare or as Paralympians. The truth is that millions of disabled people are neither, simply living ordinary lives. As there is a soft bigotry of low expectation of disabled people, disabled people need to lead the way.

This leadership skill can be used in many situations at work. Disabled people often have to be firm, otherwise they are allowing people to treat them as recipients of charity. You have to be vocal to avoid being treated as a passive object.

3. Resilience and dealing with failure

Employers are always asking in interviews: how do you deal with failure?

Disabled people often can demonstrate that despite periods of ill health, hospital visits, or ignorant comments from others, they are able to get back on their feet and demonstrate tenacity. You must also be efficient with your time when you are managing a disability, which improves organizational skills.

The fact is that most of us will move in and out of disability in our lifetimes, whether we do so through illness, an injury, or merely the process of aging.

Reasons for including disability on the diversity agenda

We are an aging population and will have to work for longer. Over time our senses and minds will change. If you stick around long enough then you will probably become a member of the disability club. We need to normalize disability, as it is a fact of life.

At any one time, one worker in six will be experiencing depression, anxiety, or problems relating to stress. In many cases, these problems lead to absence from work. The average employee takes seven days off for illness each year, of which 40 percent are for mental health problems.[1] If we are unable to speak about this at work openly, this will just further the stigma and shame surrounding mental health.

Most disabled people – approximately 86 percent – acquire their disability whilst of working age, so employers need to be able to respond to this.

People with disabilities are the biggest minority group. There are 13.3 million disabled people in the UK, with 18 percent of working age adults being classified as disabled.

People with disabilities tend to develop additional skills as outlined above: problem solving, empathy, resilience, and seeing things from a completely different angle. If you are not recruiting disabled talent, you are missing out on a large talent pool.

Tips for employers to work in a more inclusive way

I have some general do's and don'ts below, but this list is not exhaustive.

1. Attitude

If you have an open attitude to people with disabilities, your staff will feel able to embrace and express their differences freely and authentically. There is no better way to improve confidence and fulfilment at work.

A recent survey shows that it is the perception of disability which causes the majority of challenges that people with disabilities have each day. The message about recruiting and retaining disabled talent needs to be not just an afterthought but to be embedded in every aspect of the business. Is the culture in your organization open to people with disabilities? Is your website in an accessible format? What about if someone with a disability needs a reasonable adjustment for the assessment or interview? How easy is it to speak to a named person to deal with these issues? What about your front of house staff – security guards and receptionists? Have they had disability awareness training? First impressions count. Remember, you will also have clients with disabilities.

One of the simplest ways of challenging your attitudes is to perhaps take on a student who has a disability to undergo work experience at your organization. You will undoubtedly learn a lot about the different way someone needs to work and the reasonable adjustments required to put that person on an equal playing field.

2. Awkwardness

Do not define somebody by their disability. Wheelchair users, for example, have heard all the "jokes" and "lines" thousands of times – "don't drink and drive", "don't run me over", "have you got a license for that?" and "women drivers!" are some of the common ones. It is simply a lazy reference to the chair when people feel the need to say something, possibly due to awkwardness on their part. We all make mistakes, especially if we are not used to disability. If a person says something which they feel caused offence, it is best to simply apologize quickly and move on.

No one wants to be defined by one aspect of their identity. If you wouldn't do it with someone's gender, race or sexuality, disability is no different. Education is key, but the most effective way to demystify disability is to work alongside a disabled person. It is best to remember that if you don't know how to react, or what a colleague may need support with, the easiest way is just to ask!

3. Awareness

Language

Be aware of your language. An easy way to remember whether a word may cause offence or not is asking yourself: is it disempowering or empowering? The word "wheelchair-bound", for example, is banded about and is part of everyday language, but it suggests someone who is passive and disempowered.

Why is language important? Thoughts affects our words and our behavior. The more commonly accepted word is “wheelchair user”. If you are not sure of the word to use, it is acceptable to ask the person with the disability who will be able to guide you. The way you communicate with people with disabilities is powerful, as it will either alienate them or include them (e.g. “living with cerebral palsy” as opposed to “suffering from”).

One of my clients, a leading law firm, asked their employees: “Do you have a disability – yes or no?”. Only two percent of people identified with that label. They then asked: “Do you have a disability or long-term health condition?”. Around 20 percent of people felt that they belonged in that category. This enabled the firm to capture the data. It is also important to tell people why you are asking for this information and who has access to it, in order to engender trust. People with disabilities and health conditions are sometimes exchanging personal and sensitive information; it is therefore important to be open and transparent.

Some people may not consider themselves to be “disabled” (e.g. cancer, dyslexia) or perhaps there is a reluctance to be put into that box, so it is essential to use inclusive language.

Etiquette

Using the example of a wheelchair user, most chair users do not like someone leaning on their chair and treating it like a piece of furniture. You wouldn’t just lean on someone’s arm. It is an invasion of someone’s personal space.

Do not push someone without asking. Empower the individual by allowing them to approach you should they require assistance.

Opening a door will not cause offence, as you would do this for anybody. It is important not to be patronizing, as this is disempowering and reinforces the perception of having low expectations of someone who uses a wheelchair.

Kneeling down to speak to someone in a wheelchair makes some chair users uncomfortable. They feel it is patronizing, as though someone is speaking to a child. It may be more appropriate, if possible, to pull up a chair next to the person and sit down beside them, making this gesture as natural as possible. Otherwise, just talk to someone as if you would anyone if they were sitting in an office chair and you were standing by their desk. If you are not sure, it is acceptable to ask the person what they would prefer.

4. Adjustments

Some people with disabilities will need soft adjustments to enable them to work effectively with neither environmental nor attitudinal barriers such as flexible hours, rest breaks, etc.

These adjustments may change over time due to a change of medication or perhaps a fluctuating health condition; it is therefore important to check in regularly with the individual. Do staff know what adjustments are available for people with disabilities at the organization? Are they comfortable asking for what they need? Is the process of asking for adjustments straightforward, speedy and easy to navigate?

The organizations which are confident with disability and are therefore more inclusive usually have in place something called a "disability passport". A disability passport is a document that details the reasonable adjustments a staff member with health or disability issues needs at work. The passport hinges on open, supportive discussion between line manager and employee. If you are an employee who requires adjustments to support you at work, or if you are a line manager to someone who needs adjustments, a disability passport could benefit you. The purpose of the passport is mainly threefold:

- It helps individuals to have difficult conversations with their line managers;
- It forms a basis for future discussion – avoiding issues when managers change; and
- It is a good record of what has happened if there are challenges later on.

5. Aspirations

People with disabilities have aspirations like everyone else. It is important not to make people with disabilities feel just grateful for having a job, but to discuss in appraisals their goals and challenges.

Does the organization have an active disability network? If so, I would signpost the individual to this, although it is also that person's own choice whether to join the network. A disability network can perform three main functions:

- A support network;
- A consultation board for HR in respect of policies which affect people with disabilities and long-term health conditions; and
- A means of enabling disability confidence to continue to grow.

Does your organization have any role models, particularly senior staff, who speak openly about their disabilities/health conditions? They can do this via blogs on the intranet or videos. Having senior people in the organization telling their story gives others the confidence to also share. It also gives people aspiration within the organization. As the saying goes: if you see it, then you can be it.

6. Ask

Finally, don't make assumptions about people with disabilities. Simply ask. We have to watch our biases by not assuming people with disabilities wouldn't want to go on a secondment, go to court, or go and work in one of the overseas offices, for example. They could be the best person for the position, so it is therefore important not to eliminate them without even asking how this could be possible and whether it is something that they would like to do. If you shy away from the conversation it simply sends a negative message to the individual that they are not even considered suitable and are not valuable to the organization.

What are the tangible benefits?

The UK's Business Disability Forum produced a report entitled *The State of the Nation – Retaining and Developing People with Disability* (June 2015), which includes some interesting figures that can shed light on what may happen if firms fail to engage with their disabled employees.

Replacing an individual employee can cost upwards of £30,000 – an equivalent of over $42,000 at the time of this chapter being published.[2] More importantly, not only does it cost employers when an employee leaves; it also costs the organization to gain and train a new employee. On average, workers take 28 weeks to reach optimum productivity, which has an estimate median costs of £25,181 (over $35,000) per employee.[3]

Practical tips – quick wins

Disability champions

Find senior people within your business to "come out" and speak openly about their disability. Personal stories capture people's attention. Consider putting testimonial videos of people's personal stories on your firm's diversity and inclusion and recruitment pages.

Inclusive disability networks

Start disability networks, which include not only those people who have a disability, but those who have an experience of a disability so that it is not so much an "us and them" and "disabled versus non-disabled" dialogue. You will capture more people if the group is more inclusive as many people may have a child, sibling, parent, or partner, who has a disability and they can bring a wealth of experience to the group and also feel more connected to the firm.

Give visibility to disability

I am aware of a partner in a leading law firm who has a hearing impairment and has never mentioned this at work, but now recognizes that she is a role model for those who have disabilities that perhaps lack confidence or do not feel connected to their organization. Encourage others not to pull the ladder up behind them.

Just get started, get "perfect" later

It may seem overwhelming at first, as there may be so much to do in the business and you might be worried about getting it "wrong". The best thing to do is just to get started, as it at least puts disability on the agenda, which is a big statement in itself.

Diversity and inclusion is not about box ticking. It is not a case of putting things in place and expecting a diverse business to bloom overnight. It is like everything else with your business – you've got to keep working at it and approach diversity in a long-term, sustainable way.

References

1. The Sainsbury Centre for Mental Health, policy paper 8.
2. *HR Review*, February 2014.
3. *Ibid*.

Chapter 5:

The power of purpose – retaining women by promoting passion

By Karen J. Johnson-McKewan, partner at Orrick, Herrington & Sutcliffe and winner of the National Association of Women Judges' Florence K. Murray Award

The revelation

In the fall of 2017, I was in the middle of trial. It was a trial freighted with more than the usual stress: it was high-profile with significant political implications, and it was the subject of constant media coverage. A litigator for more than 30 years by then, I was familiar with the nervous stomach and adrenaline rush that comes from preparing for trial, the long hours and short sleep that trials require, and with the small but persistent voice in my head that asked me why I was working so hard, why I had chosen this work, and why didn't I just let other people do it. That voice had always been there in the lead-up to trials: whispering that there was a less stressful path open to me, and quietly undermining the choices that had led me to this place. I had always answered that voice with deferral: "I'll get through this one, and then I'll be done. I'll find something else to do." Every time, when trial was over, the voice went quiet, and I got back to work.

However, as I approached this trial, I realized that voice had been silent. For the first time in 32 years of practice, I felt no doubt about the value of what I was doing, or whether the Herculean effort it required was proportionate to the legal issues I was fighting about. As it happened, this was my first pro bono trial in many years, and it was a significant case involving an issue near and dear to my heart: access to women's health services, challenging the constitutionality of a law in a conservative state whose recently-elected governor was openly hostile to my client. Once that trial was over, I reflected on the notable absence in this trial of the whispering, doubting voice, and what it was about this case that had so effectively silenced it.

It wasn't a matter of passion for the cause; by the time I get to trial in any case, for any client, I have a strong conviction in and excitement about telling my client's story. My colleagues on this trial team were exceptional lawyers and delightful human beings, equally motivated to win the case. However, these were lawyers I knew well, and I had worked with many of them before. That wasn't it. The client was appreciative, but my favorite clients always are.

After pondering the mysterious absence of the pre-trial doubts, I came to the conclusion that the lack of internal questioning this time was the product of all of those factors – passion for the client's cause, the cohesiveness of the team, and the gratitude of the client and the people it serves. While all of those factors do generally characterize all of my work, both paying and pro bono, in this case, the passion arose from a vivid sense of social value intrinsic to the case we were litigating, and a sense that my team and I had the power – with our training, intellect, hard work, and support from our firm – to influence a result that could be life-changing for people who could not do this for themselves.

Because I am also passionate about finding ways for women attorneys to enjoy long and satisfying careers – ideally, free from the internal doubts that I have long endured – I wondered whether there might be some way to harness this experience for the benefit of my female colleagues.

Damming the departures: what isn't working

That question comes from hard and lonely experience: women make up at least half of US law students, but they drop out of the profession earlier and in greater numbers than men. At major American law firms, women represent just 19 percent of the equity partners. It's much worse for women of color: they represent just 18 percent of the women equity partners nationally, and two percent of the equity partners overall.[1] Despite law firms' increasing focus and investment on recruitment, retention and promotion programs targeting women, those percentages have remained stubborn for a very long time.

Anyone participating in law firm diversity programs over the years will recognize the cycles that have worked their way through the profession. At first, we all thought the women who were leaving did so because they found it impossible to reconcile the demands of a full-time legal career with their child-bearing and child-rearing responsibilities. In response, law firms lengthened maternity leaves and created part-time programs. That may have stemmed part of the tide, but even with those programs women continued to leave law firms in greater numbers than men.

Focus on sexual harassment education and stricter enforcement of anti-harassment policies in law firms followed, and then programs on unconscious or implicit bias. Firms also re-examined their compensation systems to assure equivalent treatment of similarly situated men and women and minorities. Law firms started elevating women in greater numbers into some firm leadership positions, and when they realized that time spent in leadership was time taken away from business development work, those same firms built business development training programs for women. In short, law firms have tried everything they can think of to fix structural inequities in their firms, to instill a greater sense of inclusiveness, to be aware of unconscious bias, and to help women build their practices. And yet, we are still stuck at around 18–20 percent of equity partners in large law firms.

Moreover, we also know that some of our early thinking about why women leave the profession was not entirely correct. While it is true that women tend to leave the full-time practice of law in their child-bearing years more than men of the same vintage do, what we missed in the data is that women disproportionately leave the law much later, too: in their 40s and 50s.[2] To what do those women attribute their departures?

First, as it turns out, not all firms are as effective as they think they are in their inclusion programs or in addressing implicit bias. Women still cite a sense of ongoing unfairness around law firm recognition of their contributions, both economic and cultural; a lack of flexibility in how they do their work; and the lack of a welcoming and inclusive culture.[3] However, there are consultants who are focused on every one of those areas, making as much or as little headway as the culture of the law firms they serve will permit.

A different question: why do women stay?

These oft-cited reasons for women's dissatisfaction with their careers in law firm, however, fail to account for the fact that the women who do stick with the practice of law for the long term are living in the same ecosystem with the women who leave. The women who stay presumably suffer through the same unfairness, the same lack of flexibility, and the same non-inclusive culture. Given those headwinds, the more interesting question to me is this one: why do we stay?

To begin to answer that question, I developed a hypothesis based on my last trial experience. Several features of that experience supply the foundation: there was great social value in that work; I shared that sense of a greater purpose with my highly motivated, extremely talented colleagues; my client and the people my client serves were appreciative of our efforts; and we understood that we were able to deliver those high-quality legal services to people who could not otherwise afford them because of the training and support we received from our firm.

When I returned home after the trial, I started looking for evidence in social science research that might support the notion that some or all of these characteristics account for the longevity of the legal careers for some women. If the data supported that notion, the next question became how we might reframe our thinking and our discussions about *all* of our work in a way that might lead more women to stay.

The promotion of passion

There is data to support the notion that women in particular have an acutely-felt need to be useful: according to the Center for Talent Innovation, fully 80 percent of US women surveyed reported that it was very important for them to "reach for meaning and purpose" in their careers.[4] Women queried in that study described "meaning and purpose" as having work that effects a lasting impact on others, both inside and outside of their professions. Those researchers also found that "women are significantly more likely than men (57 percent vs 35 percent) to say that the ability to contribute to the wellbeing of society is very important to them in their work/career".[5] They went on to say that "the most engaged working women are those who see their careers furnishing them the platforms and agency to advance the causes most important to them".[6]

The Energy Project and Harvard Business Review conducted a survey in 2014 of nearly 20,000 employees, and reported that 36 percent of those who found meaning in their work were more than twice as likely as others to report being satisfied in their jobs, and were over 90 percent more engaged at work.[7] Moreover, in a 2015 Deloitte survey of about 7,800 millennials (defined as college-educated full-time members of the workforce born after 1982), 60 percent described "a sense of purpose" as "part of the reason they chose to work for their current employers".[8] In its 2017 survey, Deloitte reconfirmed that finding (and a similar conclusion from the 2016 survey), and noted that "employees who feel their jobs have meaning, or that they are able to make a difference, exhibit greater levels of loyalty".[9] In my own decidedly ad hoc research, whenever I've floated the idea with other women that they are likely to remain more committed to the practice of law so long as they feel they are "useful," or better yet, "socially useful," I have been met with consistent agreement. The idea seems to resonate.[10]

Finding meaning and purpose in the practice of law

Assuming this is an important piece of the puzzle for retaining women in law firms, the challenge then becomes what law firms can do to leverage that need into conditions that lead to greater longevity and success for women in the practice of law. Law firms that find ways to inculcate their culture with these principles should find greater success in both retention and recruiting of women. Because the research strongly suggests these needs are felt not just by women, but by millennials more broadly, the changes aimed at improving and lengthening the careers of women should also inure to the long-term benefit of the firm with all of its employees.

Instilling a greater sense of purpose in the work of a law firm must happen in at least three areas: billable client work; pro bono work; and other externally-facing community participation. Of these, the most challenging is the first category.

Billable client work

How to help attorneys in large law firms find meaning and purpose in the work they do every day for paying clients will vary widely from one practice area and attorney to another. In some practice areas, the social value intrinsic in the work will be obvious: supporting the business of renewable energy companies is an easy example for lawyers interested in the environment. Likewise, public finance lawyers can find great satisfaction in knowing they participated in the development of bonds whose sale proceeds help build schools, airports, and bridges (my own firm points with great pride to the Golden Gate Bridge in San Francisco as a project our forebears' work helped to finance). Litigators can find satisfaction in telling a story well and persuasively, especially when they believe in the work their clients are doing, or in defending the honor of the individuals they represent.

However, even in these examples, while the lawyers leading the engagement may feel a sense of privilege to be trusted with the client's weightiest challenges, it is not always quite so keenly felt at more junior levels of the teams. Even if the matter is strategically important for the company, the work that our associates sometimes find themselves doing (e.g., document review, diligence checklists, etc.) does not always feel to them like strategically valuable work. Moreover, with some clients, even matters that are strategically valuable to the company may not feel socially valuable to our associates if they don't have a deep understanding of the company's business, or the reasons the company is pursuing the deal or waging the litigation battle.

For the lawyers toiling away on the minutiae of transactions or litigation matters, for whom the big picture feels inaccessible, sources of inspiration can be difficult to find. It therefore falls to the leaders of those engagements to assure that all of their team members feel the inspiration, and understand how their work feeds the larger goals of the engagement. Team leaders in these circumstances must develop a narrative to assure that their associates appreciate the multiple ways that the work they are doing is valuable. At one level, they need to understand that they are using and developing unique skills that will further their own personal growth, and help them to advance to more complex tasks. At another, they also need to understand how their contributions are essential to the client's cause (e.g. "I know document review is hard, but I'm counting on you to find the crucial facts in those documents, which will help to frame our strategy, and our client's story").

Of course, we all know that lawyers vary widely in their ability to lead and inspire their colleagues, and that different firms have different expectations about what sorts of behaviors they reward. For any firm interested in harnessing the power of purpose to retain their female lawyers, it must approach this work intentionally and methodically. Among other things, these firms must:

- Instill a greater sense among its partners that how they talk about the work associates do and the work we all do for our clients has an impact on retention of associates, particularly women and minorities. Law firm leadership should encourage partners to:
  - talk about their clients' work as part of our society's overall economic and social structure, and understand that doing so is important to our associates' feelings of commitment to the firm and to our clients' work; and
  - talk to associates about how their skills and unique strengths are bringing value to the client, as well as how the assignments they do fit into the larger strategy and objectives for the matter;
- Build similar themes and narratives into training programs as associates move through the ranks and begin overseeing and training more junior attorneys; and
- Develop externally-facing programming in which we invite attorneys and clients to engage in discussions about the importance of finding purpose and meaning in our work, and invite our clients to share their stories about why they do what they do, and why they find it important and valuable.

Pro bono

With respect to pro bono legal services, the connection between legal work and a greater social purpose is obvious. Nevertheless, many firms deliver a mixed message to their lawyers about pro bono work. While acknowledging their lawyers' professional responsibility to serve the community, many firms also make clear that associates should not overdo the pro bono work lest it interfere with the billable work those associates are also doing (and which pays the bills). This is an essential message – law firms are for-profit enterprises, after all – but it should be delivered in a manner that makes clear that the firm is looking for overall balance, and not suggesting that its lawyers need only perfunctorily clock pro bono hours for the sake of qualifying for the American Lawyer's "A-List".

Instead, firm leadership should highlight and celebrate its lawyers' pro bono work internally and externally, at every opportunity. It should formulate programs that facilitate work on high-impact pro bono matters, and encourage that work as a reward to those who have made significant firm contributions. On such matters, any focus on the economic need to maintain balance between pro bono and billable work should be measured at the firm or practice group level, not at the individual lawyers' level, to assure that those enjoying the reward of working on a matter that promises no financial benefit to the firm also understand the firm stands firmly behind them in that work.

In short, given the direct benefit to the firm that pro bono work can deliver in the form of improved retention of women (and, more generally, of millennials), internal messaging around pro bono must be shifted: rather than an economic burden for the firm to shoulder, major pro bono undertakings should be treated as a reward for great work. Those same significant pro bono matters can also be leveraged as training opportunities for young lawyers, and a chance for lawyers who share a common passion for the client's cause to collaborate.

Community work

Like pro bono, work that lawyers do in the community – serving on boards, participating in community activities, engaging in and promoting charitable work – has obvious social benefit. It is not, however, something that many firms make an effort to promote. Many corporate entities ask that their senior executives serve on the boards of charitable organizations, and use those connections to build opportunities for community involvement among employees. Many corporations also send groups of employees out to engage in full days of community work (often accompanied by significant corporate donations to the selected organizations). Charitable organizations benefit, and the employees benefit by the team-building experience and the sense of having spent their time supporting important community work. Law firms can and should emulate those corporate practices by (1) requiring members of their leadership teams to affiliate with a community group of their choice; (2) organize community service days for practice groups or offices, either with community groups selected by leadership members, or by popular vote; (3) include community focused team-building projects at all firm retreats; and (4) build robust internal and external messaging around that community work, to build an internal *esprit de corps* and to facilitate recruiting.

Conclusion

The data (not to mention my own experience) support the proposition that women are likely to feel more loyal to the institutions that employ them, and to remain longer in the practice of law, when they feel meaning and purpose in the work that they are doing. When their law firms give them inspiration for their client work, reward them with meaningful, high-impact pro bono work, and actively encourage them to participate in their communities in a manner consonant with their passions, they will stay. And they will inspire more women to join that law firm.

References

1. American Bar Association, ABA Presidential Initiative on Achieving Long-Term Careers for Women in Law, Report on the National Summit Held at Harvard Law School, November 7-8, 2017, at 5. Full report may be found here: https://www.americanbar.org/content/dam/aba/administrative/office_president/womeninlawsummit_harvard_finalreport.authcheckdam.pdf
2. *Id.*
3. *Id.* at 7.
4. Sylvia Ann Hewlett and Melinda Marshall, "Women Want Five Things," at 27 (12/9/2014), Center for Talent Innovation. Executive Summary found at: http://www.talentinnovation.org/_private/assets/WomenWant percent20FiveThings_ExecSumm-CTI.pdf.
5. These researchers surveyed 5,309 college-educated respondents in the US, UK, and Germany between the ages of 21 and 64 currently employed in certain white-collar occupations.
6. *Id.* at 28.
7. *Id.*
8. Melanne Verveer and Kim K. Azzarelli, "Fast Forward: How Women Can Achieve Power and Purpose," Houghton Mifflin, 2015, at p. 23.

9. "Mind the gaps. The 2015 Deloitte Millennial Survey" (2015), found at https://www2.deloitte.com/content/dam/Deloitte/global/Documents/About-Deloitte/gx-wef-2015-millennial-survey-executivesummary.pdf
10. "The 2017 Deloitte Millennial Survey; Apprehensive millennials: seeking stability and opportunities in an uncertain world." Deloitte, 2017. Found at: file:///C:/Users/k32/Downloads/gx-deloitte-millennial-survey-2017-executive-summary.pdf
11. Two of the research studies cited here – the Deloitte and Harvard Business Review surveys – do not differentiate between men and women. Moreover, the Deloitte study focused entirely on millennials, male and female.

Chapter 6:
The basics and beyond – how to raise the bar for LGBTQ diversity in the legal profession

By Wesley D. Bizzell, president-elect of the National LGBT Bar Association and senior assistant general counsel for Altria Client Services

Over the past few years, I have been privileged to visit numerous sites that were important in the struggle for civil rights in America – Central High School and Daisy Bates' home in Little Rock; Brown Chapel AME Church and the Edmund Pettus Bridge in Selma; Medgar Evers' home in Jackson; the 16th Street Baptist Church and Kelly Ingram Park in Birmingham; the Dexter Avenue Baptist Church and parsonage in Montgomery; the Dr. Martin Luther King, Jr. Historic District in Atlanta; and many others. During these visits and in my conversations with those who were on the front lines fighting for equality, I was often reminded of Margaret Meade's inspiring observation: "Never doubt that a small group of thoughtful, committed citizens can change the world. Indeed, it is the only thing that ever has." As we mark the 50th anniversary of the assassination of Dr. Martin Luther King, Jr., we also celebrate Dr. King as well as the brave men, women and children who marched bravely, advocated eloquently, and – despite tremendous odds – magnificently changed the US and the world, helping to bend the moral universe's arc towards justice.[1]

Even today, that arc still must be bent. While much progress has been made over the past decades, much work remains to increase diversity, inclusion, and equality in both corporate America and the legal community.[2] Consequently, we still need thoughtful and committed individuals dedicated to ensuring that our society and our workplaces are welcoming to all individuals, including those who identify as lesbian, gay, bisexual, transgender, and queer (LGBTQ). In my experience, most companies, law firms, and their leaders are thoughtful and want to support their LGBTQ employees. However, they may not fully understand the workplace challenges faced by this community or how to address them.[3]

Unfortunately, no single policy, program, or practice will solve the lack of LGBTQ representation in corporations and law firms. In fact, all of us who are involved in this work know it is not a destination that we finally reach one day. A company is never going to be able to complete the "task", check the box, and move on. In contrast, achieving diversity, inclusion, and equality is a journey that has multiple milestones.

This chapter begins with the basic policies, programs, and practices a company or law firm should adopt to attract and retain LGBTQ employees. It also discusses how to go beyond those basics to forge a better, more inclusive, and more authentic corporate culture that truly embraces all diverse employees, including those who identify as LGBTQ. However, these efforts must be integrated into the organization's business and day-to-day activities. In order to succeed, such efforts cannot simply be bolted-on; other groups of employees cannot be an afterthought. Instead, they have to be rooted in the organization's culture, coupled with the organization's overall business strategy, and treated as a business-critical priority.

Where we are

Over the last 50 years, countless articles have been written providing the business case for diversity, including LGBTQ diversity.[4] In fact, a Google search for "business case for diversity" yields over 27.1 million hits, many of which offer compelling and persuasive data on the benefits of a diverse and inclusive workplace. I will therefore not focus on the multitude of reasons that diversity, and in this case LGBTQ diversity, is vital for an organization's success. That said, it is important to note our starting points – that LGBTQ individuals (along with other diverse individuals) are woefully underrepresented in the senior management of corporations and in the partnership ranks of law firms, and LGBTQ animus and discrimination in the workplace continues to exist.

The US Commission on Civil Rights estimates that between 5.4 million and 8.2 million employees self-identify as LGBTQ, with the vast majority (85.33 percent) working in the private sector.[5] However, in corporate America, the number of LGBTQ CEOs and general counsels in the Fortune 500 can be counted on a single hand, and less than one half of one percent (0.03 percent) of directors of Fortune 500 companies are openly LGBTQ. For law firms, only 1.99 percent of law firm partners identified as LGBTQ in 2017.[6]

Unfortunately, but unsurprisingly, many LGBTQ individuals also continue to face discrimination in the workplace, at rates much higher than other groups of employees. According to a report published by Out & Equal in 2017:

- One in four LGBTQ employees has reported they experienced employment discrimination in the last five years;
- 27 percent of transgender people who held or applied for a job in the last year reported being fired, not hired, or denied a promotion due to their gender identity; and
- Nearly one in ten LGBTQ employees has left a job because the environment was unwelcoming. [7]

Clearly, LGBTQ individuals continue to face challenges both in our society at large and in the workplace.[8] The intersectionality of race, gender, and ethnicity makes these statistics even more troubling. LGBTQ employees of color face significantly higher rates of discrimination than their white counterparts.[9] Thus, it is not surprising that the Out Now Global LGBT2020 Study, which surveyed more than 100,000 LGBTQ individuals, found that 24 percent of lesbians, 30 percent of gay men, 40 percent of bisexuals, and 55 percent of transgender employees in the US believed that coming out could negatively impact future promotions.[10] A groundbreaking study of the legal profession, currently being conducted by the American Bar Association in partnership with Syracuse University's Burton Blatt Institute, will shed additional light on the challenges facing LGBTQ lawyers in both law firms and corporate law departments.[11]

Further, all of us who are LGBTQ know that coming out is not a one-time occurrence. LGBTQ individuals come out throughout their careers. Coming out happens every time we change jobs, meet new colleagues, secure new clients, or move to a new office location. For us, it occurs when we place photos of our spouses or partners on our desk and when we discuss our weekend plans in casual conversations with colleagues. The willingness of LGBTQ employees to be authentic in such situations hinges on how they believe their boss, their colleagues, and their clients will react. Sadly, too many LGBTQ employees read the situation and conclude it is necessary to hide their sexual orientation and gender identity in the workplace. A 2016 report from Credit Suisse states that 41 percent of LGBTQ workers in the US and 72 percent of senior LGBTQ executives say they have not come out openly at work.[12] Such covering is harmful to both the employee and the organization, detrimentally affecting individual employee morale, engagement, and retention.[13]

As a result, it remains important for all law firms and corporations to examine their practices, policies, and procedures to ensure that they are not only welcoming of LGBTQ employees, but that those employees can grow, thrive, and advance in their careers within that organization.

Advancing to the basics

Even today, a large number of companies and law firms are just beginning the journey for diversity, inclusion, and equality as it relates to their LGBTQ employees. Although it may appear to be an overwhelming task, there are a number of immediate steps a company or law firm can take to intentionally and proactively foster an inclusive and welcoming culture. Although these steps may be simple, they can quickly engender extremely positive outcomes.

Inclusive workplace policies

The starting point for any corporation or law firm should be examining its existing non-discrimination and anti-harassment policies to confirm the policies specifically cover LGBTQ employees. While some states and localities have enacted workplace protections for LGBTQ employees, the vast majority of jurisdictions have no such laws in place. As of 2018, only 20 states explicitly provide workplace protections on the basis of gender identity, and 22 on the basis of sexual orientation.[14]

Thus, it is crucially important that an organization's policies clearly and specifically prohibit discrimination and harassment based on a person's real or perceived sexual orientation, gender identity, or gender expression. Thankfully, most large organizations already have such inclusive workplace policies. According to the 2017 Human Rights Campaign's Corporate Equality Index, 91 percent of the Fortune 500 have a non-discrimination policy that includes sexual orientation, and 83 percent have a policy that includes gender identity.[15]

Commitment from leadership

As a compliance attorney, I frequently cite "tone at the top" to describe the importance of senior management in promoting ethical behavior and creating a culture of compliance. Likewise, a law firm's or corporation's leadership must be passionate and outspoken advocates for diversity, inclusion, and equality. Leaders must visibly walk the talk, or their employees will conclude that these ideals are not truly valued by the organization.

Parity in benefits for LGBTQ employees

Another foundational element is LGBTQ-inclusive benefits. Three areas should be specifically examined: benefits for transgender employees, fertility treatment for same-sex couples, and parental leave policies for same-sex couples.

For employer-provided healthcare benefits, all transgender exclusions should be removed, and clinical guidelines should permit coverage for mental health counseling, hormone therapy, medical visits, surgical procedures, and other treatments related to gender transition. An increasing number (58 percent) of the Fortune 500 are now comprehensively providing transgender-inclusive health care coverage.[16]

Additionally, same-sex couples who are utilizing fertility treatments to create a family are often treated differently than heterosexual couples because insurance policies routinely require a medical diagnosis of infertility. While a same-sex couple may not be clinically infertile, they nonetheless are unable to biologically conceive a child together. Removing this infertility requirement makes conception services available to all employees, including same-sex couples. While many companies have not yet embraced this change, Intel and Johnson & Johnson are two companies leading on this issue.[17]

Many same-sex couples build their families through adoption or surrogacy. An organization's parental leave benefits should be provided to all new parents – maternal, paternal, adoptive, or surrogacy-assisted – regardless of how the family is formed.

Diversity webpage

A company's or law firm's efforts on diversity, inclusion, and equality are of limited value if the organization is not communicating those efforts to its workforce and the public at large. When those efforts are not internally and externally publicized, many will doubt the organization's commitment to a truly inclusive workplace. A regularly updated, comprehensive webpage not only informs current employees and job candidates, but it also celebrates the advances the organization is making. One best practice is for the webpage to include metrics related to diverse employees, data on supplier diversity efforts, highlights of its diversity-related recruitment activities, and information on the organization's strategic diversity initiatives.

Expansion of the talent pool

A company or law firm must broaden its recruitment strategy if it seeks to have a diverse talent pool. A number of LGBTQ organizations host annual recruitment opportunities, including the National LGBT Bar Association's Lavender Law Conference, the Out & Equal Workplace Summit, and the Reaching Out MBA Career Expo. A law firm or corporation can also sponsor networking opportunities with LGBTQ organizations at area universities and law schools or with local LGBTQ bar associations.[18] Of course, data tracking must be a part of such outreach to ensure measurable improvements in diverse hiring are occurring.

Education to equip management

Many corporate leaders, even those who consider themselves "progressive," may not be fully knowledgeable about the LGBTQ community. For example, when discussing the "Q" in LGBTQ, I am often asked: "Isn't the term queer offensive?". Knowledge is powerful, and the more leaders understand the LGBTQ experience, the better allies they can become.

To address these types of issues, my company's LGBTQ employee resource group (ERG) recently partnered with a local organization to create a voluntary "LGBTQ 101" workshop for executives, and we have reached over 85 percent of company executives just in the first four months of 2018. After providing basic information about the LGBTQ community, participants are asked to imagine themselves as various types of new LGBTQ employees (i.e., a transgender employee, a lesbian employee, and an employee who is gender non-conforming). They are then asked to imagine what would they hope for, what they worry about, and what the individual would want in order to feel welcome. It has been a powerful workshop that both educates and evokes empathy.

Going beyond the basics

While the basic policies, programs, and processes highlighted above demonstrate a commitment to a diverse and inclusive workplace, organizations need to move beyond mere commitment. Organizations must ensure they are actually hiring, retaining, and promoting diverse talent. Aspirations and commitments are important but are not sufficient.

Establishment of an LGBTQ employee resource group

Creating an LGBTQ ERG will reap multiple benefits, if thoughtfully structured. ERGs are employee-led networks where members join together based on shared demographic factors such as gender, race, ethnicity, or LGBTQ status. ERGs can help drive change and foster a diverse and inclusive workplace, while at the same time helping the organization meet its business objectives. Thus, effective ERGs cannot merely be social networks. If the company or law firm is too small to sustain specific ERGs, a more general diversity ERG might be a satisfactory alternative.

ERGs are a vital component to demonstrating a commitment to diversity, inclusion, and equality. However, they are not a panacea; ERGs cannot be the sole entity within the organization advancing diversity and inclusion policies, programs, and processes. While ERGs have an extremely important role to play, senior management cannot abdicate responsibility for diversity and inclusion to ERGs. ERGs should serve as a catalyst for change, be thought leaders on diversity and inclusion, and be a sounding board for senior management, but ERGs should not be seen as the only advocates for cultural change. Leadership needs to step up too.

A successful ERG allows employees to be valued, engaged, and challenged to contribute to the organization.[19] This creates networking and leadership opportunities for these diverse employees and also provides greater visibility with and access to senior executives. Because it allows LGBTQ employees to be a more visible part of the culture, it encourages LGBTQ employees to, as DeRay Mckesson describes it, "come out of the quiet".[20] In this way, an ERG allows LGBTQ employees who have been quietly out at work to also be visibly out, where they are seen and heard as their full, authentic selves.

As one of the founders of my company's LGBTQ ERG, I have witnessed first-hand the power of an ERG to create a better, more inclusive, and more authentic corporate culture. The ERG has empowered my company's LGBTQ employees to be more visible, and it has encouraged sometimes difficult but always necessary conversations about difference, intersectionality, sexual orientation, gender identity, and gender expression. As importantly, it has inspired allies to stand up and be counted as caring about diversity and inclusion for LGBTQ employees.

One of the recent activities of my company's LGBTQ ERG beautifully illustrates these points. Last year, the ERG published a short booklet that contained various employees' coming out stories; this year, we turned those stories into short podcasts. A longtime employee used this as an opportunity to come out to her colleagues, something she had never previously done in her decades with the company. After the publication of this woman's story, an ally told us how inspiring these coming out stories were and how they moved her to be a more vocal and visible ally. Another employee told us how these stories gave her the courage to come out to her supervisor and her colleagues. An active LGBTQ ERG can be a powerful force for cultural change within a company and a law firm, tremendously benefiting both straight and LGBTQ employees.

Leadership accountability

The leadership of corporations and law firms must not only be vocally supportive of their organization's diversity, inclusion, and equality efforts, but they must also be accountable for them. One method to drive accountability is the formation of an executive diversity council, led by the company's CEO or the law firm's managing partner and composed of other senior leaders. This council sets and governs the organization's diversity and inclusion strategy and through regular meetings serves to focus leaders' time and attention on these important issues. Another more controversial but extremely effective method is incorporating diversity, inclusion, and equality requirements in the formal evaluation process for leaders, where their advancement and compensation is tied to certain diversity and inclusion milestones.

Self-identification

Although each LGBTQ employee has had his or her own diverse experience, we all have one thing in common – we have each taken a journey in order to be ready to tell others who we are. Thus, all of us understand how important it is to be yourself and be included – both in life and in the workplace. While Federal laws require organizations to capture certain information related to the diversity of their workforces, there is no requirement to obtain data about LGBTQ employees.

A best-practice in this area is asking employees to voluntarily self-identify their sexual orientation, gender identity, and gender expression. Being counted is vital to ensuring that an organization fosters a diverse workplace where everyone is able to be heard, included, and valued. A self-identification process through existing human resources systems helps an organization improve recruitment, development, and advancement of LGBTQ employees and also allows it to track progress for its LGBTQ inclusion efforts, in the same way it does for other diverse employee populations. While the data may be used for statistical analysis and tracking, personally identifiable information should always be kept confidential and should not be shared with an employee's manager or co-workers.[21]

Measurement of LGBTQ promotion and advancement

Utilizing the self-identification data, an organization must also actively monitor promotions and advancements to ensure LGBTQ employees are not being left behind. The best diversity programs cannot help someone seize an opportunity that never materializes. Thus, an organization must use data – not anecdotal evidence – to ensure LGBTQ employees are given the opportunities to progress.

Gender transition framework

Law firms and companies must welcome and embrace transgender employees who are transitioning in the workplace. To ensure this occurs, these organizations should have a clear and understandable framework on how the organization responds when an employee indicates they will transition. Understandably, this may be an enormously stressful moment for the employee, and written guidelines, created in advance, will help provide structure to support a respectful and successful workplace transition for the employee.

While the framework should comprehensively address how the company will work with an employee, it is important to remember that each employee's situation will be unique. Every step of the process must hinge on the employee's consent, and the framework should reiterate the need for privacy and confidentiality. In addition, the framework should clearly set out expectations for all involved, including, HR, management, the employee's immediate team members, as well as other colleagues.[22]

Executive leadership programs

While LGBTQ leaders face many of the same challenges as other leaders, they do so in the context of their identity as a diverse individual. For LGBTQ employees, leading as their authentic self can seem frightening, and executive leadership programs can help such individuals understand the power of authenticity.

A number of excellent leadership courses have been developed that focus on LGBTQ and other diverse individuals, including Stanford University's Graduate School of Business LGBTQ Executive Leadership Program (focusing on LGBTQ individuals who work in corporations, non-profits, and law firms) and the Leadership Council on Legal Diversity (focusing on in-house and outside counsel who are diverse).[23] A company or law firm should actively encourage high-potential employees to participate in such programs and underwrite such costs as part of the employee's leadership development. Doing so indicates that the organization is investing in its LGBTQ employees and provides an opportunity for LGBTQ employees to further develop their leadership skills and expand their network.

Philanthropy and community engagement

Companies and law firms are often involved in national and local civic organizations and bar associations. Many contribute to these organizations, volunteer, provide pro bono representation, or have employees serve in leadership roles, such as on the organization's board of directors or steering committee. Ensuring that LGBTQ organizations are included clearly demonstrates the company's or law firm's commitment to diversity, inclusion, and equality.

Supplier diversity

Supplier diversity initiatives ensure that minority-, women-, veteran- and, LGBTQ-owned businesses have access to procurement opportunities at corporations and law firms. A company's or law firm's supplier diversity efforts should specifically include LGBTQ suppliers. Since 2004, the National LGBT Chamber of Commerce has been the certification body that verifies that eligible businesses are majority-owned by LGBT individuals.[24] Of course, merely having such a program is not enough; the organization must use data to ensure the program is effectively engaging diverse suppliers.

Speaking out and standing up

A growing number of corporations and law firms are also speaking out in favor of LGBTQ equality issues and standing up when the rights of LGBTQ people come under attack. In recent years, when discriminatory legislation has been advanced at the Federal, state, or local level, many business organizations have rightfully denounced such attacks. For example, in 2016 executives from more than 100 companies, including many Fortune 500 companies, signed an open letter requesting that the North Carolina Governor repeal anti-LGBTQ House Bill 2.[25] Many (but not all) of the discriminatory provisions of that legislation were later repealed, due in part to the vocal and sustained business outcry.

Conclusion

As this chapter illustrates, there are many strategic insights and tactical actions companies and law firms can take to ensure their workplaces not only are open and welcoming to LGBTQ employees but that diversity, inclusion, and equality are ongoing business objectives and corporate obligations.[26] My hope is that this chapter serves as less of a checklist and more of a motivating guide, where individual corporations and law firms build upon these guidelines to implement concrete initiatives to achieve their own successes. While it will always be a journey, by implementing such policies, programs, and processes corporations and law firms can create positive cultural change and continue to ensure that the arc of the moral universe continues to bend towards greater justice.

References

1. As Dr. Martin Luther King repeatedly stated: "The arc of the moral universe is long, but it bends toward justice."
2. For those unfamiliar with the difference between diversity and inclusion, here is a perfect explanation from T. Hudson Jordan: "Diversity means all the ways we differ. Some of these differences we are born with and cannot change. Anything that makes us unique is part of this definition of diversity. Inclusion involves bringing together and harnessing these diverse forces and resources, in a way that is beneficial. Inclusion puts the concept and practice of diversity into action by creating an environment of involvement, respect, and connection – where the richness of ideas, backgrounds, and perspectives are harnessed to create business value. Organizations need both diversity and inclusion to be successful" (*Diversity Journal*, March 2011). A wonderful, succinct explanation comes from Vernā Myers: "Diversity is being invited to the party; Inclusion is being asked to dance".
3. While this chapter focuses on how corporations and law firms can ensure they are truly inclusive of LGBTQ employees, many of the suggestions can be applied to promote a welcoming culture for all diverse people.
4. M.V. Lee Badgett, et. al, The Williams Institute, *The Business Impact of LGBT-Supportive Workplace Policies* (2013).
5. US Commission on Civil Rights, *Working for Inclusion: Time for Congress to Enact Federal Legislation to Address Workplace Discrimination Against Lesbian, Gay, Bisexual, and Transgender Workers* (2017)
6. National Association for Law Placement, *LGBT Representation Among Lawyers in 2017* (January 2018), available at https://www.nalp.org/0118research.
7. Out & Equal, *2017 Workplace Equality Fact Sheet: Lesbian, Gay, Bisexual, and Transgender (LGBT) Workplace Discrimination at a Glance* (2017), available at http://outandequal.org/2017-workplace-equality-fact-sheet/
8. Unfortunately, the experience of young Americans does not offer much positive news either. According to a recent survey of young Americans aged 15 to 24, 83 percent of those who identified as LGBTQ report having witnessed someone being mistreated because of their gender identity or sexual orientation or to have personally experienced such mistreatment. In addition, nearly one-third (32 percent) who identified as LGBTQ reported that they personally had been mistreated or targeted because of their sexual orientation or gender identity, with a majority (56 percent) saying they feared for their safety, and roughly as many (54 percent) believing the acts were direct and purposeful. Such discrimination is often also intersectional, in addition to other discrimination based on the individual's race, gender, religion, or nationality. Public Religion Research Institute, *Diversity, Division, Discrimination: The State of Young America, an MTV/PRRI Report* (2018), available at https://www.prri.org/research/mtv-culture-and-religion.
9. M.V. Lee Badgett, et. al, The Williams Institute, *Bias in the Workplace: Consistent Evidence of Sexual Orientation and Gender Identity Discrimination* (2007), available at http://williamsinstitute.law.ucla.edu/wp-content/uploads/Badgett-sears-lau-hobias-in-the-workplace-jun2007.pdf.

10. Out Now Global, *LGBT2020 Study LGBT Diversity: Show Me the Business Case* (2015), available at http://www.outnowconsulting.com/media/13505/Report-SMTBC-Feb15-V17sm.pdf.
11. To participate in this study, visit https://syracuseuniversity.qualtrics.com/jfe/form/SV_dds9YLorbjiOlsp?id=cqjx. See also, American Bar Association Press Release, *ABA launches nationwide study to expand opportunities for disabled, LGBT+ lawyers* (May 2017), available at https://www.americanbar.org/news/abanews/aba-news-archives/2017/05/aba_launches_nationw.html.
12. Credit Suisse Environmental, Social and Governance (ESG) Research, *LGBT: The Value of Diversity* (April 2016), available at https://research-doc.credit-suisse.com/docView?document id=x695480&serialid=u0qj22TwXJAwyF%2FreBXW%2FeSFdVyYwRIZQ
GZP1IAumTo%3D.
13. For more information about such covering, see Kenji Yoshino, *Covering: The Hidden Assault on Our Civil Rights*, (Random House 2006).
14. Human Rights Campaign, *Corporate Equality Index: Rating Workplaces on Lesbian, Gay, Bisexual, Transgender, and Queer Equality* (2018), available at https://assets2.hrc.org/files/assets/resources/CEI-2018-FullReport.pdf?_ga=2.38946851.1447157528.1523037760-1813341130.1500314766.
15. *Ibid.*
16. *Ibid.*
17. Intel News Fact Sheet, *Intel Announces Industry-Leading Enhancements of U.S. Benefits; Supports Diverse Needs of Working Moms and Dads*, (October 20, 2015), available at http://download.intel.com/newsroom/kits/diversity/pdfs/Intel_Expanded_Benefits_FactSheet.pdf. Johnson & Johnson, *Helping Our Employees Build Families: Enhancing Adoption, Fertility, Surrogacy & Nursing Mother Benefits* (May 5, 2016), available at https://www.jnj.com/our-company/helping-our-employees-build-families.
18. For a listing of local LGBT bar associations, see https://lgbtbar.org/what-we-do/affiliates/.
19. Additional information on forming an ERG can be found at: Human Rights Campaign, *Establishing an Employee Resource Group*, https://www.hrc.org/resources/establishing-an-employee-resource-group; Diversity Inc., *Meeting in a Box: Employee Resource Groups* (2015), available at http://bestpractices.diversityinc.com/medialib/uploads/2015/01/Meeting-in-a-Box-Employee-Resource-Groups.pdf; Metropolitan Business Association, *LGBT Employee Resource Group Programming*, available at http://mbaorlando.org/dnii/erg; Kenneth Matos & Trenton Adams, *Best Practices For Starting An LGBTQ+ Employee Resource Group* (2017), available at https://www.lifemeetswork.com/insights-archive/starting-lgbtq-erg-workplace.
20. GLAAD, *#BlackLivesMatter Activist DeRay Mckesson Speaks at #glaadgala San Francisco* (November 8, 2015), available at https://www.youtube.com/watch?v=ZI5DHebDITU.
21. More information about self-identification can be found at: Human Rights Campaign, *Collecting Transgender-Inclusive Gender Data in Workplace and Other Surveys* (Oct. 26, 2016), available at http://www.hrc.org/resources/

collecting-transgender-inclusive-gender-data-in-workplace-and-other-surveys; Diversity Best Practices, *Self-Identification of LGBT Employees* (2015), *available at* https://www.diversitybestpractices.com/sites/diversitybestpractices.com/files/import/embedded/anchors/files/_attachments_articles/rr_lgbt_self-id.final_.pdf; Out & Equal, *Where Are Our LGBT Employees?* (2009), available at http://old.outandequal.org/wp-content/uploads/2014/12/2009-Self-ID-report.pdf; Kellan Baker, et. al, *How to Collect Data About LGBT Communities* (Mar. 15, 2016), available at https://www.americanprogress.org/issues/lgbt/reports/2016/03/15/133223/how-to-collect-data-about-lgbt-communities; Lynn Pasterny, Stonewall, *Do Ask, Do Tell: Capturing Data on Sexual Orientation and Gender Identity Globally* (2016), available at https://www.stonewall.org.uk/sites/default/files/do_ask_do_tell_guide_2016_0.pdf.

22. For more information about transgender guidelines, see: Human Rights Campaign, *Transgender Inclusion in the Workplace: A Toolkit for Employers* (2016), available at http://www.hrc.org/campaigns/trans-toolkit.
23. For more information about the Leadership Council on Legal Diversity, see: http://www.lcldnet.org/. For more information about the Stanford University LGBTQ Executive Leadership program, see: https://www.gsb.stanford.edu/exec-ed/programs/lgbtq-executive-leadership-program.
24. For more information about the National LGBT Chamber of Commerce's supplier diversity certification program, see: http://www.nglcc.org/what-we-do/diversity-inclusion.
25. Human Rights Campaign and Equality North Carolina, Letter to Governor Patrick McCrory, available at http://assets2.hrc.org/files/assets/resources/NC_CEO_Letter_(3).pdf.
26. Other helpful resources include: American Bar Association Commission on Sexual Orientation and Gender Identity, *Best Practices Promoting LGBT Diversity* (2011), available at https://www.americanbar.org/content/dam/aba/administrative/sexual_orientation/sogi_best_practice_guide_lgbt.authcheckdam.pdf; Great Place to Work and Pride at Work Canada, *Beyond Diversity: An LGBT Best Practice Guide for Employers* (2017), available at https://www.greatplacetowork.ca/images/storage/2017_white_papers/prideatwork_greatplacetowork_final_digital.pdf.

Chapter 7:
The Apollo Project – a global focus on how to create meritocratic workplaces

By Daniel K. Winterfeldt, partner at Reed Smith and founder and chair of the InterLaw Diversity Forum

Introduction to the InterLaw Diversity Forum

I founded the InterLaw Diversity Forum in 2008, originally as an inter-organizational forum for all LGBT+ personnel in the legal sector (for both lawyers, including private practice and in-house counsel, as well as non-lawyers).

Since its founding the InterLaw Diversity Forum has expanded its scope beyond LGBT+ to encompass all strands of diversity and inclusion (including race and ethnicity/BAME, disability, and social mobility), with a particular focus on cultural change in the workplace and "multiple identities"/intersectionality.

Since the launch of the InterLaw Diversity Forum, the legal sector's performance in Stonewall's Work Equality Index (WEI) has dramatically improved. In 2007 there were no law firms represented in the Top 100 Employers, and the legal sector ranked second from the bottom. In 2017, however, there were 17 law firms recognized in the Top 100 Employers, and the legal sector was the top-ranking sector overall. Indeed, Stonewall has stated: "A major part of the movement forward for the (legal) sector has been the InterLaw Diversity Forum. It helped provide a sector specific focus."

This success has encouraged the InterLaw Diversity Forum to expand its offering, some of which includes:

- Monthly panel-discussion meetings for both our LGBT+ network and our award-winning race and ethnicity (BAME) network;
- Our disability network, ENABLE, which launched in December 2017;
- The Apollo Project, an annual, cross-sector competition seeking out evidence-based examples of best practice for inclusive workplace

cultures, providing these as a free resource that other organizations can adapt to their specific needs. This is covered each year in a global special report by the *Financial Times*;

- The Apollo Leadership Institute, which is a global hub for general counsel from all sectors, and focuses on inclusive leadership and culture, diversity, and inclusion and the creation of meritocratic workplaces;
- InterLawConnect, our new cutting-edge online mentoring program, which launched in early 2018;
- The InterLaw Diversity Forum Student Lab, which connects high-potential diverse students across the UK with their peers, law firms, corporate institutions, and barrister chambers;
- Purple Reign, which is a photographic project that features LGBT+ and ally role models and focuses on intersectionality, the second phase of which is currently underway; and
- Our annual charity fundraiser, the Winter Carnival, which has to date raised over £400,000 for various LGBT+ charities.

The InterLaw Diversity Forum currently has more than 4,000 members and supporters from 215 law firms and chambers, and from 280 corporates and financial institutions.

Background to the Apollo Project: "diversity 101 isn't working"

In 2009/10, the Law Society of England and Wales conducted three diversity studies around barriers to career progression in the legal sector, each focusing on a different strand of diversity: (i) *Obstacles and Barriers to the Career Development of Women Solicitors*; (ii) *Ethnic Diversity in Law Firms: Understanding the Barriers*; and (iii) *The Career Experience of LGB Solicitors* (conducted with the Law Society by the InterLaw Diversity Forum). They are collectively referred to as the "Barriers Reports". The Barriers Reports focused on three different populations, but seemed to conclude the same thing – these diverse groups all faced similar obstacles.

The InterLaw Diversity Forum sought to follow up on this observation and designed and conducted a study that collected a wide range of quantitative and qualitative data from across the UK legal sector. In July 2012, the InterLaw Diversity Forum, with support from The Law Society and the Bar Council, surveyed almost 2,000 respondents from all strands of diversity and inclusion in the UK legal sector. From this data it published its ground-breaking report, *Career Progression in the Legal Sector.*[1] The report combined hard data with respondents' perceptions of their own career progression, as well as their perception of the fairness and transparency of policies and practices in their workplaces. The goal of the report was to identify the barriers facing these diverse groups and to provide recommendations to address and ultimately solve these issues.

InterLaw Diversity Forum's *Career Progression in the Legal Sector* was the first of a series of high-profile diversity reports to come out over the course of the next 18 months. These included (i) the McKinsey/30 percent Club "Shifting the Needle" (December 2012); (ii) the Law Society's International Women In Law Summit report "Setting the Agenda for Change" (January 2013); and (iii) the Women's Business Council report (specifically the "Getting On" section) (2013).

While these reports have slightly different scopes, they all ultimately deliver the same bad news: "Diversity 101 isn't working". Despite the efforts made by businesses and organizations to effect cultural change, there has not been significant improvement. This is a frustrating result for many organizations and their leaders who have read the reports and recognize the challenges that exist. They know there is a strong case for organizational change and better culture because it results in improved talent management and increased efficiency, as well as a better delivery of service to clients. They just need more practical guidance on what to do to make those changes.

The Apollo Project: driving cultural change for meritocratic workplaces

Research has shown that most D&I initiatives don't work. This realiza tion provided the impetus to establish the Apollo Project.

The Apollo Project is a global cross-sector initiative – launched in 2014 by the InterLaw Diversity Forum – for businesses and organizations of all sizes, which provides the practical tools needed to better embed more inclusive workplace practices and cultures to promote meritocracy and "level the playing field". It seeks out and awards ground-breaking initiatives and examples of best practice which are backed up by evidence in an annual competition, and then offers these as an "open-source" resource for other organizations to adapt and implement. Winning initiatives have provided proof of measurable outputs and can be replicated or adapted by other organizations looking for guidance in this area.

All winning initiatives are freely available on the Apollo Project website,[2] thus enabling other organizations to shape and inform their work on diversity and inclusion, talent management, and organizational change.

Individuals and organizations with winning initiatives receive an "Apollo Project: Architects of Meritocracy" award for their innovative work in instigating cultural change. Initiatives are judged by a panel based upon strict criteria, shining a global spotlight on real agents for change.

Each year, alongside the *Financial Times*' report, the InterLaw Diversity Forum publishes a Winners Book along with updates on past winners. Apollo Project sponsors have included organizations such as General Electric, Lloyds Banking Group, RBS, Walmart, CMS, and Reed Smith.

Apollo Project winning initiative: a case study for cultural change

Winner (2017): Gretchen Bellamy (Walmart)

Initiative: "Global Diversity & Inclusion Legal Profession Pipeline Integration – Latin American case study"

Overview

From 2013–15, Gretchen Bellamy served as assistant general counsel, legal operations, global diversity & inclusion in Walmart Stores, Inc's legal department. The program she spearheaded there is designed to provide equal opportunity to law students and lawyers in international markets who are under-represented in the legal profession due to race, ethnicity, gender, sexual orientation, socioeconomic status, or the like. This program is the first known instance of an international company focusing intently on diversification of one profession in this manner in places where it operates internationally.

In 2013, Ms. Bellamy led the Walmart home office legal department in the study of its own international legal departments and of its outside counsel firms in the international markets, examining diversity and inclusion in those countries. She was supported by Alan Bryan, senior associate general counsel, legal operations, Walmart; and by Gonzalo Smith, VP & general counsel, Latin American Region, Walmart. She started the project by conducting significant research about each country's stage of development in terms of diversity/inclusion country-wide, locally, and within the legal profession, as well as how those concepts impact outside counsel management and the practice of law. These efforts included extensive interviews, conversations, and collaboration with university deans and other academic partners; law firms that work with Walmart in Latin America; head-hunters specialized in the legal profession; directors in non-governmental organizations; government officials; and others. The objective was to gain a better understanding of societal and cultural implications for any Walmart-institutionalized changes to policies and procedures affecting its outside counsel.

After conducting market visits, she and the team concluded that the environment in Chile made it clear that the program should be initiated there. The conferences with external stakeholders led the team to determine that English proficiency and professional networking skills would have the greatest impact on ethnic minority and socioeconomically-challenged law students seeking good legal jobs.

As a result, Walmart's legal department pledged to provide English lessons for three years to 12 law students from the most prominent Chilean universities as well as to partner with highly reputable Chilean law firms to establish clerkships, mentoring relationships, and post-graduate employment opportunities for these students. That is the framework of this international diversity and inclusion effort moving forward, and this is a program which can be replicated in other countries (and by other corporations) depending on the specific cultural findings in each country.

Background

Walmart's legal department's commitment to diversity and inclusion is firm. It holds itself accountable internally, and it strives to hold its outside counsel law firms accountable for meeting diversity, inclusion, and flex-time goals. By doing so, it continues its commitment to creating opportunities for women and minorities within the legal profession, which will better position them to provide superior advice and solutions to the company.

In 2005, the legal department began its diversity and inclusion journey in earnest. One of its first major steps was to increase and promote the use of diverse attorneys in the legal profession by installing 40 minority and women relationship partners at its top 100 law firms. This one act resulted in the shifting of approximately $60 million of existing business to those new women and minority relationship partners.

In 2013, senior vice president & general counsel, Tim Cheatham, challenged Ms. Bellamy to gain a better understanding of how the legal offices in Walmart's international markets function and how she might be able to create an inclusive and truly global legal department. The goal was to have all global offices working toward (and achieving) similar goals based on the same parameters as they relate to outside counsel management and diversity and inclusion.

Methodology

The initiative had to be completed in a culturally sensitive way and in an appropriate time frame. Moreover, Ms. Bellamy recognized that the landscape of the legal profession is quite different in each country. As is often the case, the opportunity for the legal department to lead initiatives to make positive changes in the legal field was immense. By spearheading this initiative, it promoted a genuinely needed change in society generally, and set the bar for all other corporations – to strive for outcomes similar to what the legal department was able to achieve nearly ten years earlier in the United States.

In an effort to break down the social inclusion barriers, and working in conjunction with the top two Chilean law schools, Ms. Bellamy, the project team and the leaders of the Walmart-Chile legal department ("WM-C") identified 12 socioeconomically-challenged students rising to their third year of law school (in a five-year degree program). It was concluded that by the end of the second year, there can be an accurate assessment made of the students' ability to be successful in law school, which is why students in their third year were chosen. WM-C, with support from the Home Office legal department, is currently supporting these 12 law students by providing stipends for English language training for their last three years of enrolment.

The program was announced in October 2014 at the WM-C Superconference, which had over 250 attendees from the Chilean legal community as well as business leaders, both national and international. The process for identifying the students began in November 2014, with WM-C leaders working collaboratively with the local university. The program officially commenced in March 2015 when the new school year began.

Within four years, WM-C can modify and utilize the outside counsel guidelines ("OCGs") to request that outside counsel firms include at least one minority on Walmart matters. Within 15 years or sooner, Walmart can utilize the OCGs to ensure that a minority partner is either working on company matters or serves as the relationship partner. Currently, there are no minorities who are in such a position, and while there is not an immediate return on investment, a great impact on society will be seen in the future by increasing the number of under-represented individuals qualifying for jobs they traditionally are prevented from holding.

Finally, WM-C will start the process of collecting data for metrics similar to those used in the Home Office legal department. The OCGs should require firms to provide WM-C certain data so the WM-C team can benchmark with the Home Office and other global markets. WM-C will have the data needed to support its goal of diversity on the team of lawyers working on its matters, as well as to affect the hiring policies and actual hiring results of each firm. WM-C, with the assistance of the Home Office legal department, could then begin discussions with outside counsel firms about what it means to be an equal opportunity employer. What is needed first is the pipeline of diverse talent, which is what the legal department and WM-C are creating with this program.

Outputs

The outside counsel guidelines have been amended for each Latin American country in which Walmart operates. The legal department in each market is responsible for ensuring the implementation of the guidelines, which include commitments regarding diversity and inclusion. The program was launched in Chile, and WM-C is ultimately responsible for the implementation and success of the program. Two WM-C attorneys are responsible for working with the interested stakeholders (law firms and universities) to identify the law students who will participate as well as the law firms where those students will work as interns and finally as associates.

Six students were chosen from Pontificia Universidad Católica de Chile to participate in this groundbreaking pipeline program and began in March 2015. The additional six students from the Universidad de Chile started in November 2015. The demographic breakdown for the students from Pontificia Universidad Católica consists of four women and two men. Included in that demographic is one disabled student. The impact on the students is evidenced by the feedback received from the coaches and leaders of the program. The students are all actively engaged in their language lessons, a program that is strictly monitored. Additionally, each law firm mentor of the students has reported that the students are integrating effectively and the network for each student has expanded beyond what was anticipated. The students in the program have been successful and will be graduating from law school soon.

Feedback

The response to and recognition of this initiative has been positive, both internally and externally. The significance of the program led the project team to win the 2015 Dr. Martin Luther King, Jr. Visionary Award, which is given by the company. This award recognizes and affirms those who have made significant and tangible contributions in the areas of diversity and inclusion, justice, and human rights. Externally, the team has been approached by a number of corporate legal departments that want to replicate the program. The program has been presented by a multinational company in Mexico to local corporations. A law school dean in Costa Rica is prepared to be part of a similar program when launched. It has been recognized that the initiative cannot be sustained by the commitment of only one company, so the level of interest from other corporate legal departments is exciting, and other corporations wishing to replicate the program are encouraged to do so. Ms. Bellamy looks at the program as an opportunity to change the legal profession throughout the world by ensuring equality for all who enter it.

References

1. https://docs.wixstatic.com/ugd/5aa06e_2e32bcdbd4b04fa5b546a2d3bbae57c4.pdf
2. www.theapolloproject.net

Chapter 8: "Access to the Bar for All" – so much more than a financial assistance scheme

By Charlotte Ogilvie, marketing and communications executive at Garden Court Chambers

> *"I wear a scarf, I am a short, brown girl. I don't (yet) wear a wig. I have felt out of place in court and I often walk into courtrooms and everyone is an older white man wearing a wig. It used to be intimidating, but I'm getting used to it. Through 'Access to the Bar for All' I can see that I am welcome here and that I am supported."*
>
> Nazia Islam, participant from Oaklands School, Tower Hamlets, London

Race, gender, or socio-economic background should not act as barriers to inclusion; yet today women, people from Black Asian and Minority Ethnic (BAME) and low socio-economic backgrounds remain under-represented at the Bar. In 2017 in the UK, women accounted for 36.5 percent of barristers, and only 13.7 percent of QCs (Queen's Counsel) – a designation given to eminent lawyers who have proven excellence in advocacy. Only 12.2 percent of barristers are from BAME backgrounds, and only 6.4 percent of those were QCs in 2017. At this rate, it would take 50 years before women comprised half of all QCs and 100 years for the percentage of BAME "silks" – a colloquialism for a member of Queen's Counsel – to mirror the general population. This is unacceptable.

In 2017, in an effort to redress this imbalance and accelerate the rate of progress, Garden Court Chambers set up "Access to the Bar for All", a long-term mentoring scheme which encourages students from minority and disadvantaged groups to consider a career as a barrister. Nazia Islam, one of six young women in our first cohort, believes that diversity schemes are necessary to encourage and support people from all sections of society, and especially those who aren't always able to enter the legal profession without them. Islam maintains that they will not only benefit the individuals taking part, but the legal profession and justice system more widely. She says, "We need to have more women representing women on women's issues, and more practitioners from diverse backgrounds representing the diverse communities that make up our country."

It is not in our interest for the Bar to be dominated by people from one background alone. A diversity of experiences and outlooks are needed and people from underrepresented groups must be shown that the legal sector wants to actively encourage and support them. If anything, people who have faced hardship tend to be more driven, committed and dedicated than their privileged counterparts. There are so many groups that the Bar hasn't warmed up to yet, where raw materials are left untapped and undiscovered from a lack of proactive pursuit. This is changing, and must continue to do so.

What sparked the scheme?

In November 2016, Garden Court Chambers won an award for public and administrative law. Leslie Thomas QC – chair and joint head of Garden Court Chambers, who attended the awards ceremony – reported seeing less than a handful of black faces in a room of almost 300 people. That same month, Garden Court held an open day for potential pupils and it became apparent that those from certain socio-economic backgrounds had no experience in chambers, no contacts, and no support to remedy this.

Mia Hakl-Law, our Director of HR and Operations, and Connor Johnston, one of our barristers, respectively decided that, in order to address the under-representation of women, ethnic minorities, and people from low socio-economic backgrounds, young people needed to be approached before they decided the legal profession was not for them. They felt that a positive impact could be had if high school students had access to mentors when they were 16, before their A-levels (pre-university exams in the UK), that would offer them a helping hand over a long period of time.

Setting up the scheme

On realizing that for change to happen we would have to do it ourselves, Mia put forward a proposal at Garden Court Chambers' AGM in January 2017 which was voted through unanimously. The proposed scheme was for small-scale, full support for two students each from three schools in some of the most economically deprived areas of London: Tower Hamlets, Southwark, and Greenwich. At least one of the two young people selected from each school had to be a girl, and at least one had to come from a BAME background. All participants had to be in receipt of Free School Meals, be the first generation in their family to go to university, and live in an area that is in the top 10 percent of the Multiple Index of Deprivation. The participants were selected through a formal recruitment process run by Chambers.

The successful candidates were then offered mentoring from a barrister for five years, three weeks of paid work experience per year, and the opportunity to be awarded a £7,000 scholarship to assist with living expenses for each year of university if they went on to study a law degree at undergraduate level.

After the scheme was voted in, Mia sent out a message asking for six tenants to commit to volunteering as mentors over a five-year period. Twenty barristers volunteered within 30 minutes.

"I thought it was a fantastic idea to have a scheme that was very concentrated on a handful of mentees, but long term that would give very concrete practical and financial support to young people from specific backgrounds," says Di Middleton QC, barrister at Garden Court Chambers, who is involved in the scheme. "It's very special to be able to make such a substantial difference to one person's life. This is not just a leg-up in a financial year for an organization. It is a massively influential scheme with tangible benefits for the participants in their actual development and in their introduction to adulthood... One of the things I like about the scheme is the fact that we choose carefully where the mentees come from and let class and economic background feature in it – not just more obvious inequalities like ethnicity or gender."

Funding the scheme

The cost is spread across all members of Chambers over a five-year period. Since its inception, Garden Court Chambers has operated the Special Fund, a unique source of funding within the legal profession. Every member of Chambers contributes financially to the Special Fund through a percentage of their yearly earnings. It primarily makes donations to small, progressive, cutting-edge organizations doing legal, campaigning, or charitable work in defense of civil liberties and/or access to social justice. All funds for "Access to the Bar for All" come from this resource.

The application process

When it was agreed that the scheme was going ahead, three schools had to be chosen. Mia contacted schools which, in previous years, had asked Garden Court to take students for work experience; she also contacted the National Union of Teachers, seeking recommendations of which areas in London to aim for in terms of deprivation levels. She then pitched the scheme to a number of schools, who responded positively to her initial call. The final three were then selected based on the levels of interest and proactivity from the heads of sixth form,[1] including how successful they had been in getting students interested and involved in the introduction sessions that she had delivered.

A group of barristers in Chambers devised an application form which was sent to schools for interested students to fill in. They had to fulfil the criteria mentioned above, but also respond to questions about their motivation and current affairs.

The application forms were then assessed, and the most promising candidates were invited to Chambers to attend a formal panel interview. For most of the young people who made it to the interview stage, it was a novel experience.

Joey Liu, currently in Year 13 at Walworth Academy, Southwark, reflects on her experience of the interview: "It was the scariest thing... The questions were unexpected. It sounded daunting beforehand, but when it came around, the barristers were really friendly. They just wanted to get to know us and find out if we were the best candidates for the scheme. It was actually quite therapeutic just to have someone asking me questions and making me reflect on why I really want to do this."

The scheme

Mentoring

All participants are paired with a barrister who will be their mentor for the duration of the scheme. Mentors provide participants with someone to interact with on a regular basis outside of their normal spheres. One of the students on the scheme, Joey Liu, says: "It's good to have someone to talk to – not your parent, not your teacher, not your friend, but someone outside of it all who doesn't know you, but you get to tell them things, learn from them, exchange ideas, and it's just between you."

All mentors and mentees keep in contact by phone and email, and most pairs meet face-to-face roughly every two months. Nazia's mentor is Ann Osborne, a family lawyer at Garden Court. "Ann and I meet up. We message each other... We talk things over quite often, and I keep her posted with the latest on my university applications. It's good to have someone outside of my loop to discuss things with and she often gives me new perspectives that I might not otherwise have considered."

"We must put our money where our mouth is, and the scheme offers meaningful financial support," says Di Middleton QC. "Initially the money seemed like a really important benefit. Yes, it's part of it, but it's so much more than a financial assistance scheme."

She believes that what has even greater weight and makes "Access to the Bar for All" so unique is the long-term relationship and the exposure that comes with it. There is a "constant channel" between the mentee and their mentor, Chambers, and the Bar more widely. Giving someone the opportunity to "knock about" in Chambers, to meet barristers, attend social functions, go into court, and to have someone on the end of a phone or an email who is invested in them is invaluable. "Being in the environment and growing comfortable with it is so much part of this scheme. It's amazing to see someone becoming less and less self-conscious, and being able to really properly give hands-on help. I've seen Joey develop into someone gleaming with confidence."

Joey worked with her mentor, Di, on her application for university, stating that the constructive criticism offered, along with Di's ability to ask the right questions, was fundamental in forming a personal statement that Joey said really "sounded like me". Based on her application she was given conditional offers to study law at the University of Exeter or the University of Warwick, both prestigious universities in the UK. In her personal statement, after a discussion with Di, Joey wrote about the differences between court proceedings in immigration tribunals and criminal law, which made an impression on her. "Tribunals are held in rooms like classrooms, but criminal courts are huge, old-fashioned, and much more what you might expect. I noticed that there's such a massive difference and wondered if that represented the importance attributed to immigrants in this country. It's almost as if they're not given enough attention, or their cases aren't valued as much. It's not just the physical scenery though, but also the Home Office. I could really feel the hostile environment."

Connor Johnston is a "satellite mentor". This means that he has not been assigned a mentee, but instead offers support with more ad hoc mentoring duties such as providing mock-interviews for university. Nazia benefited from this support and had a trial run before her interview to study English Literature at Cambridge. "It was very tailored… It's different to being interviewed by your teachers who you know almost too well. The reality is that when you do go to the interview you don't know the people sitting in front of you. Having a fresh face asking me questions I didn't expect was so helpful. Afterwards, he also gave me feedback on what I needed to improve and praise for the things that I was already doing well. I realized that an interview doesn't have to be stressful, or tense. Interviewers are not trying to trick you – they are trying to bring out the best in you."

Connor, reflecting on the experience, said, "She didn't need much coaching. The most useful thing I could do was give her validation. She hasn't had any awards to show her she's brilliant, but she has all of the raw materials she needs – all she was lacking was a bit of reassurance that she was good enough."

Work experience

"There is no substitute for a working knowledge of what a job actually entails," says Mike Higgins, head of sixth form at Walworth Academy. "It's motivating and they are excited by that. They are excited by the real job." Each participant follows three weeks of paid work experience for the duration of the scheme. This is flexible and varied dependent on their interests. Joey Liu gained experience of cases regarding black markets, the use of weapons, murder, family disputes, and immigration, stating that the effort made by the barristers to really get her involved in trials has "given [her] a real insight into how things actually work". Tomi Adagunodo – currently in Year 13 at Walworth Academy, Southwark, and Nazia from Oaklands School – also saw a wide spread of different proceedings during their work experience. Hannah Dalton, head of sixth form at Oaklands School, emphasizes: "Lots of law firms and chambers offer work shadowing, work placements or e-mentoring, but for students like ours being dropped into a company for one week is not going to change their mindset or perspective in any long term or meaningful way."

Nazia commented that being so close to cases has helped her make a view of the law itself, and not just the legal profession, and develop a deeper understanding of the mechanics of the system: "It's so useful working with people who are instructed in cases every day – being able to witness them, react to them, be curious and ask anything you want, to get answers to your questions straight away and discuss them with someone who is so knowledgeable… That's something that I haven't been able to find anywhere else."

During the work experience, participants also spend time with a range of barristers who are not their mentors. This is a chance for them to grow their contacts and be exposed to a broader group of practitioners working on different areas of law. Joey said of this aspect, "I feel that this program has enabled me to build up my network… It has helped me grow in confidence and I find it so much easier to communicate with people now… I've learned how to be professional… and feel like I've become an adult as part of the process." Similarly, Tomi says, "Since starting at Garden Court my communication skills have improved and I know how to target my speech and pitch things at the right level. I'm more adaptable now, more confident and more engaged with current affairs."

Wider exposure

"On my first day of work experience, I went to Luton Crown Court. I was the only girl there and the only black person. It's quite shocking to see the lack of ethnic minority practitioners at the Bar. It's usually the ethnic minorities who are the defendants and that's really sad," says Tomi. However, being part of the scheme, she has got to know several women from ethnic minority backgrounds working in the law. "I remember shadowing Ann Osborne. She's black. I could identify with her. It was inspirational to meet someone like me in a job like this, and a profession like this. I think it's important to be able to see people who look like you, who sound like you, and who come from the same background."

Nazia commented on the position of women within the profession and suggests that it is not women themselves but the structure of the legal profession that doesn't always create the kind of space that they need. "It's disheartening, but it makes me more determined," she says. "I love that this scheme is aimed at girls – it's been amazing being around such intelligent women, both my peers and my superiors. I just feed off them. It's great to have such impressive role models – especially women from similar backgrounds to me – and I've met quite a few already. Every time I see one particular barrister at Garden Court Chambers I'm just so inspired. She is exactly what I picture when I think of a successful, confident woman: the way she is in court, how she talks to people – that's what I want to be like. I want to be just as strong."

How other chambers or firms can help widen the scheme

"For what you're able to achieve and the help you're able to give the participants, the financial impact on Chambers is really minimal," says Di Middleton QC. "It's such a substantial scheme and it doesn't need to take away from anything you might be doing already. It's possible for small chambers to take on something similar to make a difference to individuals' lives. If every chambers took on even one young person and carried them through university – whether through mentoring, work experience, or financial assistance – imagine how many people could be helped and the impact that it would have." It could easily be a daunting prospect for a set of chambers or a firm to start up their own initiatives without any guidance. Garden Court is keen and available to help advise others on setting up something similar to promote diversity, and effect wider change within the legal sector.

"The program is a huge stepping stone for people interested in law," says Joey, "and it should definitely be taken on by more chambers and firms. There are so many people who want to succeed, but there aren't always these opportunities for them to grab onto. I think that the only way we can make the legal sector more balanced is by actively seeking out BAME students."

One of the benefits of "Access to the Bar for All" is that it is small and manageable, making it affordable and achievable, not just for large organizations. The main hinge upon which the scheme turns is the fact that all lawyers involved as mentors are volunteers, which means that a chambers' or firm's costs are not massively increased by their engagement. "There is no financial incentive for them," Joey explains, "but they should be motivated to educate younger people from different backgrounds who don't necessarily have a whole system behind them. Sometimes young people like that – like me – need that extra support."

Hannah Dalton, Oaklands School, said: "There are very few schemes, currently, which recognize the many barriers faced by young people when applying for the Bar, such as being closed out by well-connected, fee-paying contemporaries and the overwhelming costs of university and the Bar course. Garden Court Chambers' scheme is so good because it recognizes that one-week shadowing schemes, common across the legal field, have little impact on increasing diversity at the Bar as they don't address the issues faced by young people from underprivileged backgrounds. The longer view taken by this scheme is crucial because the barristers provide support to students beyond the sixth form as they make choices at university, where typically there is little specialized guidance available."

There is an overrepresentation at the Bar of those who attended fee-paying schools, and barristers are more likely than not to have at least one parent who went to university. We hope that many other chambers and law firms will follow suit and will set up their own long-term schemes to address the lack of diversity at the Bar and tap into the rich vein of talent available from underrepresented groups, who have so much to offer the legal profession.

Mia Hakl-Law, Director of HR and Operations at Chambers, is happy to be contacted in relation to the scheme and offer guidance, provide further information or answer any in-depth questions.

Garden Court is thrilled and honored to have won the Chambers Diversity Initiative of the Year at the UK Diversity Legal Awards in November 2017 for our long-term mentoring scheme.

Reference

1. Sixth form refers to the final two years of secondary education (high school) in England, Northern Ireland and Wales, where students prepare for their A-level (or equivalent) examinations.

Chapter 9: Guidelines for corporate engagement – external LGBT+ issues

By Todd Sears, founder and principal, Out Leadership, and Matt Fouracre, manager, client relations and public policy, Out Leadership

Introduction

It was just seven years ago, at the very first Out Leadership Summit in 2011, that multiple CEOs from major companies came together to talk publicly about LGBT+ inclusion, and to express support for marriage equality. Since that time, corporations have taken on a leading role in driving forward LGBT+ equality, both within their companies' walls and around the world.

In 2013, the American business community spoke out forcefully for LGBT+ equality, when 278 companies, including many of the largest and most influential in the United States, signed on to an *amicus* brief to the United States Supreme Court in support of Edie Windsor's successful case to overturn Section 3 of the Defense of Marriage Act. Two years later, 379 employers joined an *amicus curiae* brief in *Obergefell v. Hodges* and urged the court to affirm the right of same-sex couples to marry nationwide. In both cases, Out Leadership partnered closely with law firms and advocacy groups to organize our member companies to sign on to the briefs and firmly establish themselves at the forefront of LGBT+ inclusion.

In the nearly three years since marriage equality became the law of the land, businesses have increasingly been called upon to take action around issues of LGBT+ equality. From where we sit, in between law firms, corporations and LGBT+ advocacy groups, sometimes it seems the volume of requests companies are receiving to take action around external LGBT+ issues have increased exponentially since *Obergefell*.

In 2016, corporations were asked to speak out against anti-LGBT+ bills in places like Georgia, North Carolina, and Texas. Last year, almost 150 discriminatory laws relating to LGBT+ issues were introduced in state legislatures. Businesses have been encouraged to join State-level corporate coalitions organized around the principles of inclusion and equality, and CEOs are often asked, and sometimes pressured, to sign open letters or otherwise speak out when laws are put forward that could negatively impact LGBT+ people.

Lawsuits around LGBT+ issues did not stop with *Windsor* and *Obergefell*. Corporations have been asked to sign-on to *amicus* briefs at various levels of the appellate process, from State Appeals Court to the United States Supreme Court, on issues including the rights of trans students, the interpretation of Title VII to include sexual orientation, and alleged conflict between the First Amendment and laws prohibiting discrimination in the provision of goods and services.

The business community is being asked to speak out on LGBT+ issues for an important reason: it can have a major impact.

Corporate opposition to Georgia House Bill 757, which would have allowed faith-based organizations to deny services and make hiring decisions based on sincerely-held religious beliefs, was a key factor in Governor Nathan Deal's decision to veto the legislation in 2016. After the bill was passed by the state legislature, hundreds of companies joined Georgia Prospers, an organization based on the premise that diverse and welcoming workplaces and communities are an integral component to healthy, thriving 21st century economies; a number of major employers specifically called on the governor to veto the bill.

Similarly, corporate pressure led to policy change in North Carolina. Businesses' opposition to the state's House Bill 2, which placed restrictions on what bathrooms trans people could use, kept the issue at the forefront of the news for months after the bill was passed and signed by Governor Pat McCrory, and helped lead to his defeat in the 2016 gubernatorial election. Subsequently, many of the most onerous restrictions contained in the bill were repealed.

Internationally, in 2017 a number of major financial services companies publicly supported the plaintiff in the QT Case, which challenged a Hong Kong Immigration Department decision to deny a spousal visa to the legally-married same-sex spouse of a British visa-holder. While the Court of Appeal did not allow the financial institutions to officially file a brief on the case, the action taken by the financial institutions was widely covered in the press and the court eventually unanimously ruled that QT should be granted a dependent visa.

While the impact of corporate engagement on LGBT+ equality is clear, it is unfortunately impossible for businesses to always take action on these issues, especially given the increasing volume of requests companies receive to speak out on a growing range of important social issues, both within the United States and around the world. Companies need help navigating these issues, and non-profit and advocacy organizations need to better understand the way companies decide to act.

That is why Out Leadership has produced guidelines for corporate engagement around LGBT+ issues.

To create the guidelines, Out Leadership convened a working group that included representatives from Out Leadership member companies as well as from companies outside our network, and select representatives from LGBT+ advocacy groups. The group discussed various models that businesses have implemented to evaluate and respond to requests for action on LGBT+ equality. We have distilled conversations from the working group into the following best practices, in the hope that they that can provide a framework for businesses to use to engage on LGBT+ equality.

As an organization uniquely situated at the intersection of law firms, corporations, and LGBT+ advocacy groups, we have observed well-intentioned organizations struggle to meaningfully engage around external LGBT+ issues. We believe that these guidelines provide a useful framework through which corporations can maximize their impact.

In general, the guidelines for corporate engagement around LGBT+ issues outlined above can also be applied to requests that companies receive to engage around non-LGBT+ social issues. While certain additional considerations may need to be addressed around more controversial potential issues, the guidelines provide a framework with which companies can initially consider requests.

Common requests

Recent requests for companies to take action around an external LGBT+ issue, whether made by nonprofits and advocacy groups, members of the public, or employees, fall into four primary categories: *amicus curiae* briefs, business coalitions, public statements, and lobbying.

Amicus Curiae briefs

In certain legal cases, a Court of Appeals will allow outside parties to submit *amicus curiae* briefs. In recent years, advocacy groups have requested that businesses sign on to corporate or employer *amicus* briefs at the levels of state appeals and supreme courts, US circuit courts, and the US Supreme Court. These briefs are typically drafted and filed by major law firms in partnership with a nonprofit or advocacy group. Usually briefs are filed on cases that are going to be argued in court; however, occasionally briefs have been submitted to a court asking it to grant *cert*.

Signing on to an *amicus* brief can be more time-consuming and complicated than other ways of taking action, as signing on to a brief requires the attention of legal counsel as well as the engagement of government and public affairs leaders within the company.

Following the Supreme Court decisions on the Defense of Marriage Act and marriage equality, companies have been asked to sign briefs on a number of cases. Some notable examples include the following.

Gloucester County School Board v. G.G.

This case asked whether Title IX protections from sex discrimination in educational programs included protections for transgender people. Among other claims, the 53 companies that signed on to this brief argued that school policies that discriminate against transgender students have adverse effects on their employees' transgender children and employees who are themselves transgender, and that such policies negatively impact employee recruitment efforts. The US Supreme Court reversed its initial decision to hear the case after the Trump administration withdrew trans-inclusive Department of Education Title IX guidelines that had been put in place by the Obama administration.

Zarda v. Altitude Express

The *amicus* brief in *Zarda* argued that it was in the interest of business for sexual orientation to be included in interpretations of Title VII employment protections. This brief was signed by 50 companies and filed to the US Court of Appeals for the Second Circuit, where the court ruled *en banc* that Title VII protections do encompass sexual orientation. The case is expected to be appealed to the US Supreme Court.

Masterpiece Cakeshop, Ltd. v. Colorado Civil Rights Commission

A total of 37 companies signed on to this brief, which argued that providers of goods and services should not be exempted on the First Amendment basis of free speech or freedom of religion from broad-based nondiscrimination laws that include protections on the basis of sexual orientation. The case was heard by the US Supreme Court in December 2017 and a ruling is expected in the spring of 2018.

Business coalitions

In a number of instances when state legislatures have considered or passed anti-LGBT+ legislation, businesses have organized coalitions around the idea that state law must be non-discriminatory in order for the economy to thrive. This approach has been most successful in

Georgia and Texas. In other cases, companies or CEOs have signed open letters organized by advocacy groups to expressly oppose discriminatory laws. Notable examples include the following.

Texas Competes

In 2015, Texas Competes launched with a pledge signed by nearly 200 companies arguing that Texas' workplaces and communities needed to be diverse and welcoming of LGBT+ people for the state to effectively compete economically. With the introduction of anti-LGBT+ legislation in the 2017 legislative session, including a so-called "bathroom bill", the coalition organized to oppose the measure, releasing a study that found that the bill had already cost the state $200 million in bad publicity. Over 1,350 companies are now members of the coalition.

North Carolina Business Leader Open Letter & Investor Statement

In March of 2016, 106 business leaders signed an open letter, organized by the Human Rights Campaign and Equality North Carolina, calling on Governor Pat McCrory and the leadership of the North Carolina General Assembly to repeal HB 2, which had overturned local LGBT+ nondiscrimination ordinances and barred transgender people from using the restrooms that corresponded to their gender identity. The letter claimed that HB 2 made it harder for companies and universities to recruit and retain talented workers and top students. Concurrently, a group of investors managing a combined $2.1 trillion, led by Trillium Asset Management and assisted by Out Leadership, released a statement calling for the bill's repeal. Later in 2016, Governor McCrory lost his reelection campaign, HB 2 was partially repealed in early 2017.

Public statements

A company or CEO may wish to release a public statement expressing support for the LGBT+ community or opposing anti-LGBT+ developments. This can be done in lieu of (or in addition to) signing on to an *amicus* brief or business coalition; it can also sometimes be the only option for a company to take a public stance on LGBT+ equality in the absence of a pending court case or business coalition. This option can also give a company the opportunity to make a broader statement around the importance of inclusion, rather than address a controversial issue head-on.

Marc Benioff

On 25 March 2015, Salesforce CEO, Marc Benioff, tweeted that the company might be forced to scale back its investment in Indiana if

Mike Pence, who was then the governor, signed the state's "Religious Freedom Restoration Act", which would have allowed companies and organizations to discriminate against LGBT+ people. After Pence signed the bill, Benioff tweeted that he would cancel programs that would result in Salesforce employees and clients traveling to Indiana. Benioff was an early and prominent critic of the legislation, leading other major employers and regional chambers of commerce to speak out against it. The law was eventually partially repealed.

Lobbying

Internal or external stakeholders might ask that companies engage with legislators and policy makers through lobbying efforts. Depending on the situation, connecting directly with lawmakers around the business and talent impact of LGBT+ inclusion can be an effective way to either complement or substitute for more public actions like releasing a statement or joining a business coalition.

Best practice framework for evaluating requests

Based on conversations with a number of companies that have engaged publicly on issues relating to LGBT+ equality, Out Leadership has distilled the following best practices for how companies can best handle requests. These best practices can also serve as a guide for nonprofit and advocacy groups, or LGBT+ employee networks, who may wish to engage a company to take action.

Guidelines

Given the volume of requests that companies receive to take action around external social issues, many companies have adopted formal checklists or decision trees through which they can evaluate potential avenues of action. Out Leadership has distilled insights from our Corporate Engagement working group into the following eight guidelines for corporate engagement.

1. Business connection

Does the issue in question have a direct connection to the company's business? Does it connect back to a company's business or to important stakeholders such as clients or shareholders?

2. Talent
Will this issue affect LGBT+ employees' willingness or ability to work in a certain location, or will the issue negatively impact colleagues' LGBT+ children or immediate family members?

3. Location
Does the company have an employee footprint in the jurisdiction affected by this issue, or are there plans for future growth in the location?

4. Impact
If this is a local issue, has it attracted attention outside its immediate locale, and will taking action lead to wider attention and positive market or talent impacts?

5. Industry Stance
Have major industry peers and competitors taken or are likely to take action on an issue, and will the company be conspicuously absent?

6. History
Has the company previously taken a public stance around an identical or very similar issue, and what are the consequences of not taking action again?

7. Alternatives
Is there an alternative action that a company can take that would be more effective and impactful, or that more closely aligns with company goals?

8. Result of inaction
What might result from not taking action around each particular request: will failing to take action negatively impact talent, shareholders, clients, or the company's brand?

Process ownership
Companies should have a clear procedure by which corporate engagement requests are evaluated, the first step of which should be to have a defined, senior-level "owner" of such requests. Because taking action on an external LGBT+ issue often requires approval from various departments, designating a single person who owns the process who can shepherd requests to other internal stakeholders is often necessary. As a best practice, an owner (or one of multiple owners) should be a

senior decision-maker, to ensure that feedback from other stakeholders is received quickly.

As government affairs, public affairs, and diversity and inclusion functions are often integral to the internal approval process, designating a process owner who sits in one of those departments makes sense for many companies. Some companies manage these requests through their LGBT+ employee network. In those instances, it is again a best practice to have the buy-in and close involvement of a senior business leader.

For one multinational corporation that participated in the working group, requests around external engagement around LGBT+ issues are managed by the firm's head of federal government affairs. As a senior leader at the company, and with the support of the company's CEO, she is able to effectively liaise between stakeholders such as the legal department, public affairs, and the firm's LGBT+ employee resource group, which ensures that the company can respond nimbly to requests.

CEO and senior leader engagement

It is much easier for companies to take action around external issues if the CEO and/or other C-suite business leaders are active allies and advocates for LGBT+ equality. Engagement at the most senior level of a company can often result in action, even if the criteria outlined in the above guidelines are not met.

As an example, we spoke with a major multinational financial services company that was a vocal opponent of HB 2 in North Carolina. Besides a smattering of financial advisors, the company did not have a major presence in the state, in terms of both employees and clients. Many of its direct competitors did not speak out against the bill or join various coalitions to oppose it. The company's head of wealth management, however, was an ally of the LGBT+ community and believed strongly that the firm needed to speak out. The company subsequently signed on to an investor statement organized by Trillium Asset Management and Out Leadership, which explained that HB 2 was bad for business and called for its repeal.

Note for advocacy groups

The guidelines outlined above are what Out Leadership has identified as best practice for businesses seeking to evaluate requests to take action around external LGBT+ issues. While no single company specifically considers all of these criteria, every company we spoke with considers some of them. Advocacy groups may find that taking these considerations into account when they make requests of companies can help speed the process along.

International considerations

While the specific requests and processes around *amicus* briefs described above are unique to the United States, companies are often asked to make public statements, lobby governments, participate in the legal process, or otherwise advocate for LGBT+ equality internationally.

Based on our conversations, we believe that the framework for engagement described earlier can also be applied to requests for engagement around LGBT+ issues in foreign countries. For companies seeking to engage around LGBT+ equality at the international level, it is helpful to consider the following.

1. The economic and business impact

To help companies understand the economic impact of LGBT+ exclusion abroad, Out Leadership has created CEO Business Briefs for 16 countries. These briefs, which also provide talking points around the business case for LGBT+ equality, can serve as a resource for companies seeking to engage abroad.

2. Support from the Head Office

For companies based in the United States, it is important for senior leaders based in the US to emphasize the business case and importance of LGBT+ inclusion when they visit overseas offices. This, along with engagement from US-based employees with local LGBT+ networks, not only provides support and assurance to LGBT+ employees abroad, but also can help alleviate potential concerns from local leaders about taking stances around LGBT+ inclusion.

3. Organizational structures

International partnerships such as law firms and some professional services firms are often not structured in a way that allows the global chair or global leadership to make decisions for the entire organization. Local partners and management often have substantial power to control budgets, employee policies and procedures, and communications. It is important for management at the global level to make sure that local and regional leaders are aware of the business and talent imperative for LGBT+ inclusion, and of the negative consequences firms can face for inaction around issues that affect the LGBT+ community.

Prior to 2017, a number of multinational companies sponsored Pink Dot, an annual LGBT+ pride event in Singapore. In 2017, the Singapore government banned foreigners from attending and sponsoring the event. As a result, a senior-level representative from a former major corporate sponsor met with the Ministry of Home Affairs, armed with an Out Leadership CEO Business Brief, and explained how supporting LGBT+ inclusive was a business driver for the company and is good for the economy overall. When the government continued to refuse foreign companies to sponsor the event, this company worked with a number of their local clients to ensure that sponsorship continued for the event.

Amicus brief best practices

Given the more complex and time-consuming nature of joining an *amicus* brief, there are a number of guidelines that advocacy groups and law firms should take into account when attempting to engage companies as *amici*.

1. Timing of outreach

Companies should be made aware of the opportunity to sign on to an *amicus* brief as early as possible. When a law firm is driving the process of writing the actual brief, it is a best practice to have them looped in for any initial outreach that is being done by advocacy groups or external partners. For major cases, the process of creating a brief will begin months before the filing deadline – advocacy groups and law firms should jointly begin reaching out to potential *amici* at the beginning of the process, not the end.

2. Process

When advocacy groups and law firms reach out to companies to invite them to participate in an *amicus* brief, they should be prepared to share an explanation of why the brief is being created, an outline of the argument, and a timeline spelling out when companies can expect to review a draft of the brief, as well as when the final brief needs to be filed.

3. Partnerships

No single advocacy group has a monopoly of contacts at corporations that might be interested in signing on to an *amicus* brief. If one particular advocacy organization is leading the process of bringing on *amici*, it is a best practice to loop in other groups that regularly engage with the private sector around these issues, to ensure that companies that might have otherwise signed on are not left uninformed of opportunities.

Common pitfalls

Many businesses take LGBT+ inclusion very seriously, and take steps to ensure that their LGBT+ and ally employees feel comfortable at work and in their communities, to the furthest extent they are able to do so. In our conversations with business leaders, however, we identified a number of pitfalls that make it difficult for companies to engage externally around LGBT+ issues. Addressing these areas can make it easier for nonprofits and advocacy groups or LGBT+ employee networks to successfully request corporate action.

1. Volume of requests

Companies now receive a high volume of requests for engagement around a wide variety of social issues. According to one senior executive, in the last year, "issues that once popped up every five years are now coming up every five minutes". For LGBT+ issues in particular, our working group hypothesized that it might be more effective for a single, widely acknowledged organization like Out Leadership to position itself as a clearinghouse, responsible for funneling requests from various stakeholders to businesses.

2. Timing

While companies are often asked to take actions or make a statement around a breaking news issue, the issue of timing is (or ought to be) less acute with regard to slower-moving legislative processes and *amicus* briefs. In these cases, companies should be given as much time as possible to evaluate a request. Companies report that they often only receive one or two weeks' notice when they are asked to sign onto *amicus* briefs, which is not sufficient.

3. Bureaucracy

Without a senior leader, particularly from the business side, pushing to move requests among internal stakeholders, things can often get bogged down at various stages of approval. Actively engaging senior business leaders is a very effective way to ensure that requests for action are not caught up for too long in the bureaucracy that often exists inside complex multinational corporations.

www.ingramcontent.com/pod-product-compliance
Ingram Content Group UK Ltd.
Pitfield, Milton Keynes, MK11 3LW, UK
UKHW021848150926
8657IPUK00005B/144

9 781783 583263